BETTY CROCKER'S
COOKING
AMERICAN STYLE

A Sampler Of Heritage Recipes

Golden Press/New York
Western Publishing Company, Inc.
Racine, Wisconsin

Photo credits appear on page 160.

Fifth Printing, 1978
Copyright © 1975 by General Mills, Inc., Minneapolis, Minnesota.

Printed in the U.S.A. by Western Publishing Company, Inc.
Published by Golden Press, New York, New York.
Library of Congress Catalog Card Number: 75-34817

Golden® and Golden Press® are trademarks of Western Publishing Company, Inc.

CONTENTS

INTRODUCTION

A collection of American recipes is a little like the friendship quilts women all over the country used to sew. Each friend gave something of her own, so that the finished quilt was full of personal memories stitched into a colorful design.

This book, too, is filled with memories. Good cooking from many places and backgrounds has contributed to the great variety in our culinary heritage. Region by region it is perhaps impossible to define American cooking, but when favorite recipes are gathered in one book, many overall characteristics do begin to emerge, like the pattern in a quilt. Side by side we find catfish cooked in a small farmhouse in Georgia and Cioppino assembled in a San Francisco apartment. We find Hasty Pudding from New England and Corn Oysters from the Midwest. Even a glance through this group of American recipes is proof of the two outstanding qualities of American cooking: the legendary American ingenuity and the diversity of influences. From this wide array we've chosen a sampler of American favorites, as appealing today as they were in the region or time they originated.

The people from all over the world who settled America brought their own food customs and, often, seeds in their pockets or sewn into their clothes. Somewhere in this huge new country they found a climate or a landscape that reminded them of home. They planted their native produce and reproduced their favorite recipes. With inventive substitutions for what was not available, the recipes gradually accommodated themselves to the new land. Children and grandchildren raised on the American versions of their parents' traditional ethnic foods are usually surprised when they travel to their ancestors' homeland. The well-loved breads, pastas or desserts are not the same there. Like the people, the recipes became naturalized Americans.

Ethnic and regional specialties are still a strong part of our evolving style, but now the variety of foods available throughout the country makes it possible for us to reproduce any recipe we desire. The continuing thread in our patchwork is the lucky abundance of vegetables, dairy products, meats and grains throughout our history. This abundance, as much as the diversity of the settlers, has influenced the extensive variety we continue to enjoy.

Almost anything can be grown in at least one of the fifty states, and with our shipping network, North Dakotans enjoy fresh artichokes from California, New Yorkers appreciate the tender Carolina okra and spring asparagus arrives in still-frozen Michigan almost as fresh as when it left Florida. Modern growing and storage techniques have made the limitations of season and place almost obsolete. Alaskan crab is very much at home in Missouri, and some of the most ephemeral berries travel all over the country both in and out of season.

The abundance and choice we take for granted today actually began after 1840. Until then fruits and vegetables were limited to their short growing seasons and were available only in their special locales. Since all food was thought to have the same nutritional value, there was no widespread interest in elusive vegetables. Nourishment meant one thing: quantity! But suddenly in the 1840s a new and important word, *iceman*, came into general use. Along with the icebox in the kitchen came the railroad cars bringing fresh produce, seafood and meat to the cities. One of the first such systems ran along the "pea shore" of New Jersey and picked up seasonal vegetables and fruits for New York City.

The perfection of the canning process at about the same time also helped revolutionize the American diet. By the end of the Civil War the soldiers, who had first tasted canned seafood, corned beef and vegetables in army camps, spread the word all over the country. From then on, ships, Conestoga wagons and households were stocked with rows of "tins." The era of convenience had begun.

More than anything else, the expansion of the railroad in the West sped this era of variety in foods on its way. After the 1880s the refrigerated railroad cars that crisscrossed the country supplied Americans with still more fresh beef and pork. Later, irrigation of the great valleys of California made a perpetual growing season for many fruits and vegetables.

These changes were rapid. The rural household stocked with root vegetables, salted meat and a barrel of cider evolved in little more than a few decades into our demanding kitchens that take for granted foods from all over the country and the electric appliances that help us prepare them.

Today, cooking demonstrations on television, more leisure time, easier world travel and fine cooking equipment give American cooks their sophisticated approach to food.

One result of this new sophistication is a renewed appreciation for our own heritage, a rediscovery of the best eating traditions of American households. We've begun to value the unique aspects of our cooking history, especially the experimental and adaptive attitudes American cooks always have had.

That was so of necessity. The very first transactions between the Indians and the English settlers seem to have involved food—the corn, squashes and beans native to America. These versatile vegetables and the game and seafood plentiful along the New England coast became the foundation of American cooking. Over 350 years later, the most definite culinary heritage we feel is for the foods that carried the English settlers through those first few winters. A pungent pot of baked beans, a pumpkin pie fragrant with spices, creamy clam chowder, the colorful mixture of limas and corn—these still are rich in our memories.

We are a long way from the frugal cupboards of colonial days. Far enough in fact that many cooks are reviving the old skills of preserving fruits, baking breads and making sausage. Often in our nostalgia for the time when food was "natural," when pickles lined the kitchen shelves and the house was filled with the warm smell of freshly baked loaves, we forget the long hours of drudgery our great-grandmothers put in to produce those foods. Even a quick look at antique cookbooks, with their advice about various agues and chills and their herbal cures and purges, reminds us of the different household skills involved at that backbreaking time. It's not hard to imagine that any great-grandmother, given the choice, would opt for easier cooking methods.

Our rediscovery of American culinary traditions, then, is from the long viewpoint of progress. With our modern appliances and supermarkets, we are free to enjoy fully the preparation of early American dishes and to continue to experiment with food in the best tradition of American cooking. Perhaps it is from this point on, now that the flow of immigration has slowed, that American cooking will take new directions. After all, our history is very short, and it took hundreds of years for other cuisines to develop.

The development of American cooking thus far has been well documented. In 1796 Amelia Simmons wrote *American Cookery*, the first book to include native foods. Ever since then cookbooks have been flourishing publications both nationally and locally. Women's organizations always have made and sold collections of recipes, not only as a way to raise funds, but from a desire to share good food. *Betty Crocker's Cooking American Style* continues in that tradition of sharing. We have simply selected good food from American kitchens past and present. The ingredients and instructions for the recipes had to be updated for modern kitchens, and, of course, every recipe was tested thoroughly by the staff at the Betty Crocker Kitchens. Not surprisingly, the recipes evoked an enthusiastic response from both our staff and the home testers throughout the country who were delighted to rediscover these traditional favorites.

Many recipes we've included keep to the basic simplicity and naturalness of the early settlers' food. Breads, corn, seafood and relishes, particularly, hearken back to those thrifty cooks who took advantage of what was naturally available. In our own time we can learn a lot about economizing by adapting their principles. Also well represented in our collection is the hearty food of the farmlands, where cooks continued in that early habit of integrity of ingredients, bounty and wholesomeness.

From these foundations we've collected a group of America's best-loved foods. Many of the recipes are traditional, and a real effort has been made to preserve the essence of the original "receipts." Many are authentic regional specialties and some are more recent recipes that have become popular all across the country.

These recipes testify to the fact that American cooking is still innovative and adaptive. From our diverse beginnings and our rich heritage, we continue to reap an abundant harvest.

Pictured opposite.
An array of bakings from all across the country. Clockwise from top: Georgia Raised Biscuits (page 10), Midwest Chocolate Cake (page 23), Sourdough Bread (page 16), Rhubarb and Strawberry Pie (page 49) and Yellow Fruitcake (page 28).

BAKING DAY

BAKING DAY

One marvel of American cooking is the large number of baking recipes that survive from a time when the circumstances and ingredients made baking a difficult and rigorous task fraught with chance. Until 1890, cup and spoon sizes were variable, and recipes usually were no more specific than "add a teacup" or "a wine glass" or, most mysteriously, "a lump." In addition, there were no regulated ovens and often no leavening. As these baking recipes were handed down, many a cake must have emerged from the oven as heavy as lead. Before the invention of baking powder, the determination to produce a light cake often went to great lengths. One early pound cake recipe from Virginia instructs that the eggs be beaten for *five* hours before adding them to the batter. About the fate of the unfortunate cook no record remains!

In early New England, baking day centered on breads made with cornmeal or with dried pumpkin that was ground into a flour. The simplest loaf was actually a flat cake made of cornmeal, water and salt, which came to be known as "johnnycake." Cornmeal was the baker's staple, North and South. Hoecake and ashcake, similar to johnnycake, were common, and in the South spoon bread was—and still is—a popular dish made with cornmeal. All corn grown in America is of five basic kinds, and these different varieties of corn produce different meals when ground. Boone County white, a type of dent corn, produced the fine white meal Southerners preferred in their baking, while Northerners tended to use flint corn, which produced the yellow, slightly heavier meal. Early Americans always were fond of hot breads with meals.

The Dutch settlers in New York were more progressive in bread making than their New England neighbors, whose wheat crops failed in the Massachusetts soil. Missing their native breads—waffles, crullers and doughnuts—the Dutch quickly planted fields of wheat, barley and rye, then built windmills to grind the grains. Soon the New Netherlands wheat was sold to the colonies in the North and South, but the breads made from wheat continued to be special until the great wheat farms of the Midwest began pouring out their bounty in the middle of the nineteenth century.

In the West, the pioneer women, the prospectors and the chuck-wagon cooks who baked breads along the trail were cooking under the most adverse circumstances. Sourdough is a bread that became so identified with the early prospectors that they even were called "sourdoughs." Crocks of "starter" for sourdough biscuits, pancakes and loaves were kept going for years. Each time the cook used a little starter, more flour, water and salt were added to the crock and the fermentation continued. When temperatures dropped, the trail cook sometimes took the crock to bed so the cold wouldn't kill the starter.

If bread baking was tricky, fine baking was even more hazardous. The easily available coarse grains were heavy. Later perlash, a leavener derived from burned wood, was introduced for

Wheat fields seem to stretch forever across the American prairie.

baking, but many cooks refused to use it because it had a bitter taste. Finally, in the last half of the nineteenth century, there were two major breakthroughs. One was the commercial production of baking powder, which started in the 1850s. After a large advertising campaign and the publication of cookbooks by the manufacturer, suspicious housewives finally were convinced of the safety of the product, which for years had been rumored to be poisonous.

Then came the development of the milling industry in the Midwest. From early beginnings, two men, Washburn and Crosby, established the Washburn Crosby Company, which later with other interests formed General Mills.

Many cakes that were popular over a century ago are still being made today. Of course we have standardized the measurements and carefully adapted every recipe to modern kitchens. Many of the old recipes were known as "great" cakes for a reason: the enormous quantities of ingredients they called for. The recipes in this chapter keep all that was "great" except the size and effort. One of these famous cakes, perhaps the glory of the Southern kitchen, is Lane Cake, which with its strong competitor Lady Baltimore, is still a traditional holiday treat. Maple-Nut Chiffon Cake, Midwest Chocolate Cake and Boston Cream Pie are also representative of the rich legacy we've inherited from determined bakers.

Though pastry desserts are common all over the world, pies somehow seem peculiarly American. Probably this is because so many of our favorites developed here. Pumpkin pie is, of course, a native. English main-dish "pyes" of minced meats evolved in America into desserts sweetened with molasses. The abundance of fruits inspired cobblers, pandowdies, deep dish pies, tarts, dumplings—all guises for simple fruit pies. In this section we've gathered a pie-safe full of the great favorites: Apple Pandowdy, Fresh Blueberry Tart, Apple Dumplings. Our Rhubarb and Strawberry Pie and Mincemeat-Pumpkin Pie are marvelous variations on old standbys. Superb Black Bottom, Chess and Shoofly Pies are so tempting they'll make you want to revive the old farm custom of pie for breakfast.

Also in this section are cookies: Jumbles, Hermits, Joe Froggers and icebox cookies—now updated and called Refrigerator Nut Cookies. These and others are great nibbles for a lunch box or for that one thing that hasn't changed in the American kitchen—the cookie jar.

Happily, most of the rigors of baking have long since disappeared. Aided not only by ovens with thermostats, but by dependable yeast, baking powder, timers and standardized recipes, even a novice can enjoy baking. Surely there is no greater example of the heritage of the American cook than this legacy of fine breads, cakes, cookies and pies.

BREADS

DIXIE BISCUITS

2 cups cake flour or 1¾ cups all-purpose flour*
2½ teaspoons baking powder
¾ teaspoon salt**

⅓ cup shortening or firm butter or margarine
¾ cup milk

Heat oven to 425°. Mix flour, baking powder and salt. Cut in shortening until mixture looks like fine crumbs. Stir in almost all the milk. Stir in just enough additional milk to make a soft, puffy, easy-to-roll dough. (Too much milk makes dough sticky, not enough makes biscuits dry.)

Round up dough on lightly floured cloth-covered board. (If using all-purpose flour, knead about 10 times.) Pat into circle about ½ inch thick with floured hands. Fold into thirds; pat again into circle about ½ inch thick. Cut with floured 1¾-inch biscuit cutter.

Place on ungreased baking sheet 1 inch apart for crusty sides, close together for soft sides. Prick biscuits several times with fork. Brush biscuits with light corn syrup, evaporated milk, slightly beaten egg or egg white if desired.

Bake until golden brown, 12 to 15 minutes. Serve hot. ABOUT 16 BISCUITS.

*If using self-rising flour, omit baking powder and salt.
**If using butter or margarine, reduce salt to ½ teaspoon.

GEORGIA RAISED BISCUITS

1 package active dry yeast
2 cups warm water (105 to 115°)
4½ cups all-purpose flour*

1 tablespoon sugar
2 teaspoons salt
½ cup shortening
Butter or margarine, softened

Dissolve yeast in warm water; reserve. Mix flour, sugar and salt. Cut in shortening until mixture looks like fine crumbs. Stir in reserved yeast mixture to make a soft, puffy, easy-to-roll dough.

Round up dough on lightly floured cloth-covered board. Knead 20 to 25 times. Divide in half; roll each half ¼ inch thick. Cut with floured 2-inch biscuit cutter. Spread tops of biscuits with butter. Place half of the biscuits buttered sides up 1 inch apart on ungreased baking sheet. Top with remaining biscuits, buttered sides up. Cover; let rise until almost double, about 45 minutes.

Heat oven to 400°. Bake until golden brown, 15 to 20 minutes. Serve hot. ABOUT 2½ DOZEN BISCUITS.

*If using self-rising flour, omit salt.

Many of America's hot breads originated in the South, where breakfast still is not complete without ham and biscuits. On the opposite page, Crusty Dixie Biscuits with slivers of Smithfield ham make a delicate sandwich, and the soft, puffy Georgia Raised Biscuits layered with slices of ham are good for Sunday supper.

The light, sugar-crusted Yam Muffins that follow are especially good with pork dishes, as Louisiana families have enjoyed them for generations. But all of these biscuits and muffins can be thoroughly enjoyed with your favorite spread, preserve or honey.

YAM MUFFINS

1½ cups all-purpose flour*
½ cup sugar
2 teaspoons baking powder
½ teaspoon salt
½ teaspoon ground cinnamon
½ teaspoon ground nutmeg
½ cup milk
½ cup mashed cooked yams or
   sweet potatoes

¼ cup butter or margarine,
   melted
1 egg
½ cup chopped pecans or
   walnuts (optional)
1 tablespoon sugar

Heat oven to 400°. Grease bottoms of 12 medium muffin cups (2¾ inches in diameter). Mix all ingredients except 1 tablespoon sugar just until all flour is moistened. Batter should be lumpy. Fill muffin cups ⅔ full. Sprinkle ¼ teaspoon sugar over batter in each cup.

Bake 18 to 20 minutes. Immediately remove from pan.   1 DOZEN MUFFINS.

*If using self-rising flour, omit baking powder and salt.

BLUEBERRY MUFFINS

1 egg
1 cup milk
¼ cup vegetable oil
2 cups all-purpose flour*

¼ cup sugar
3 teaspoons baking powder
1 teaspoon salt
1 cup blueberries

Heat oven to 400°. Grease bottoms of 12 medium muffin cups (2¾ inches in diameter). Beat egg; stir in milk and oil. Stir in flour, sugar, baking powder and salt just until all flour is moistened. Batter should be lumpy. Fold in blueberries. Fill muffin cups ⅔ full.

Bake until golden brown, 20 to 25 minutes. Immediately remove from pan.   1 DOZEN MUFFINS.

*If using self-rising flour, omit baking powder and salt.

The early settlers learned to cook with cranberries from the Indians of the Cape Cod area, who added cranberries and nuts to their corn breads. Cakes of dried venison and cranberries, called pemmican, were a mainstay of the Indian diet.

CRANBERRY-ORANGE NUT BREAD

2 cups all-purpose flour*
¾ cup sugar
1½ teaspoons baking powder
¾ teaspoon salt
½ teaspoon baking soda ·
¼ cup butter or margarine, softened

1 tablespoon grated orange peel
¾ cup orange juice
1 egg
1 cup cranberries, chopped
½ cup chopped nuts

Heat oven to 350°. Grease bottom of loaf pan, 9x5x3 inches. Mix flour, sugar, baking powder, salt and baking soda. Stir in butter until mixture is crumbly. Stir in orange peel, juice and egg just until all flour is moistened. Stir in cranberries and nuts. Spread in pan.

Bake until wooden pick inserted in center comes out clean, 55 to 65 minutes. Loosen edges of loaf with spatula; remove from pan. Let stand at least 8 hours before slicing.

*If using self-rising flour, omit baking powder and salt. Reduce baking soda to ¼ teaspoon.

BOSTON BROWN BREAD

1 cup all-purpose flour* or rye flour
1 cup whole wheat flour
1 cup cornmeal
2 teaspoons baking soda
1 teaspoon salt

2 cups buttermilk
¾ cup molasses
1 cup raisins (optional)
Butter or margarine

Grease four 4¼x3-inch cans (16-ounce vegetable cans). Beat all ingredients except butter 30 seconds on low speed in large mixer bowl, scraping bowl constantly. Pour into cans, filling each about ⅔ full. Cover each tightly with aluminum foil.

Place cans on rack in Dutch oven or steamer; pour boiling water into pan to level of rack. Cover pan. Keep water boiling over low heat until wooden pick inserted in center of bread comes out clean, about 3 hours. (Add boiling water, if necessary, during steaming.)

Remove cans from pan; immediately unmold breads. Serve warm with butter.

*If using self-rising flour, reduce baking soda to 1 teaspoon and omit salt.

We're probably fortunate in our culinary heritage that white flour wasn't readily available in early America. If it had been, perhaps we might not have developed the wide range of recipes in our baking tradition that the use of other grains gave us.

One of these grains was buckwheat, which was immortalized in the song "Dixie": "There's buckwheat cakes and Injun batter . . ." but is even more popular in the Northwest. Another grain, rye, was also available early on. It was mixed with cornmeal to make Rye 'n' Injun, a dark bread flavored with molasses. The perfection of that rough loaf became our steamed Boston Brown Bread.

Many corn breads were named for their shapes or the way they were cooked, and these simple names are often quaint to modern ears. Ashcakes, corn pone, scratch back, hasty pudding, hoecakes, spider bread, johnnycakes and slappers are a few of the breads that were familiar to the early settlers. Another, baked grits, is made from coarse cornmeal ground from hulled corn. Traditionally, Baked Grits with Garlic Cheese accompanies turkey, quail or other game birds.

BUCKWHEAT CAKES

1 package active dry yeast	1 teaspoon salt
¼ cup warm water (105 to 115°)	3 eggs
1¾ cups lukewarm milk (scalded, then cooled)	¼ cup butter or margarine, softened
2 tablespoons packed brown sugar	1 cup all-purpose flour*
	1 cup buckwheat flour

Dissolve yeast in warm water in 3-quart bowl. Stir in remaining ingredients. Beat until smooth. Cover; let rise in warm place 1½ hours. Stir down batter. Cover; refrigerate at least 8 hours. (Batter can be kept up to 12 hours in refrigerator.)

Stir down batter. Grease heated griddle if necessary. Pour batter from ¼-cup measuring cup or tip of large spoon onto griddle. Turn cakes as soon as they are puffed and full of bubbles but before bubbles break. Bake other side until golden brown. ABOUT SIXTEEN 4-INCH CAKES.

*If using self-rising flour, omit salt.

NOTE: Unbleached flour can be substituted for all-purpose flour in this recipe.

Buckwheat Waffles: Pour batter from cup or pitcher onto center of hot waffle iron. Bake until steaming stops, about 5 minutes. Remove waffle carefully.   ABOUT EIGHT 7-INCH WAFFLES.

Whole Wheat Cakes and Waffles: Substitute stone-ground whole wheat flour for the buckwheat flour.

FLUFFY SPOON BREAD

1½ cups boiling water
1 cup cornmeal
1 tablespoon butter or
   margarine, softened
3 eggs, separated
1 cup buttermilk

1 teaspoon salt
1 teaspoon sugar
1 teaspoon baking powder
¼ teaspoon baking soda
Butter or margarine

Heat oven to 375°. Grease 2-quart casserole. Stir boiling water into cornmeal; continue stirring to prevent lumping until mixture is cool. Blend in 1 tablespoon butter and the egg yolks. Stir in buttermilk, salt, sugar, baking powder and baking soda. Beat egg whites just until soft peaks form; fold into batter. Pour into casserole.

Bake until puffed and golden brown, 45 to 50 minutes. Serve hot with butter.

JOHNNYCAKES

1 cup cornmeal
1 tablespoon sugar (optional)
1 teaspoon salt

1 cup boiling water
1 cup milk
Bacon fat

Heat cornmeal in 2-quart ovenproof bowl in 375° oven, stirring twice, 5 minutes. Stir in sugar and salt. Pour in boiling water gradually, stirring vigorously with fork until all lumps are removed. Stir in enough milk to make a smooth, slightly thick batter. Grease heated griddle with bacon fat. Pour batter from ¼-cup measuring cup onto griddle, spreading to ¼-inch thickness.

Bake on both sides until brown. Stir enough milk into batter, if necessary, to make batter easy to spread.   ABOUT 8 JOHNNYCAKES.

BROILED CORNMEAL ROUNDS

1 cup dairy sour cream
¼ teaspoon salt
¼ teaspoon baking soda

1 egg, slightly beaten
⅔ cup white cornmeal
⅓ cup bacon fat, melted

Set oven control to broil and/or 550°. Mix sour cream, salt, baking soda and egg. Beat in cornmeal gradually until smooth. Stir in 3 tablespoons of the bacon fat. Divide remaining bacon fat among 12 medium muffin cups (2¾ inches in diameter); spread up sides of cups. Place muffin pan so top is 6 inches from heat; heat until bacon fat is hot, about 2 minutes. Pour about 2 tablespoons batter into each cup. Broil until tops are brown, 6 to 8 minutes.   12 ROUNDS.

Pictured opposite.
Cornmeal is the common starting point for these three American favorites. Left: Fluffy Spoon Bread. Right: Broiled Cornmeal Rounds. Bottom: Johnnycakes.

SQUASH ROLLS

1 cup milk	1 package active dry yeast
2 tablespoons butter or margarine	¼ cup warm water (105 to 115°)
½ cup sugar	1 cup mashed cooked winter squash
1 teaspoon salt	4½ to 5 cups all-purpose flour*

Heat milk, butter, sugar and salt until butter is melted. Cool to lukewarm. Dissolve yeast in warm water in 3-quart bowl. Stir in milk mixture, squash and 2 cups of the flour. Beat until smooth. Mix in enough remaining flour to make dough easy to handle.

Turn dough onto lightly floured surface; knead until smooth and elastic, about 5 minutes. Place in greased bowl; turn greased side up. Cover; let rise in warm place until double, about 1½ hours. (Dough is ready if an indentation remains when touched.)

Punch down dough. Shape into 1-inch balls. Place 3 balls in each of 24 greased medium muffin cups (2¾ inches in diameter). Let rise until double, 30 to 45 minutes.

Heat oven to 400°. Bake until light brown, 15 to 20 minutes.   2 DOZEN ROLLS.

*If using self-rising flour, omit salt.

Tortillas, breads with a Mexican heritage, are eagerly enjoyed at this San Antonio fiesta.

On the unsettled American frontier, every traveler carried a crock of sourdough starter for bread and flapjacks. Today, however, Sourdough Bread is almost synonymous with San Francisco. Booths at the airport sell the long paper-wrapped loaves to departing travelers much as stations at the edge of the desert sell gas.

As our recipe proves, it *is* possible to bake a good loaf at home, though without a humidity-controlled oven it's impossible to duplicate exactly the crusty loaves sold along the wharf.

SOURDOUGH BREAD

1 cup Sourdough Starter (page 17)	3 tablespoons sugar
2½ cups all-purpose flour*	1 teaspoon salt
2 cups warm water (105 to 115°)	¼ teaspoon baking soda
3¾ to 4¼ cups all-purpose flour*	3 tablespoons vegetable oil
	Cold water

Mix Sourdough Starter, 2½ cups flour and 2 cups warm water in 3-quart glass bowl with wooden spoon until smooth. Cover; let stand in warm, draft-free place 8 hours.

Add 3¾ cups of the flour, the sugar, salt, baking soda and oil to mixture in bowl. Stir with wooden spoon until dough is smooth and flour is completely absorbed. (Dough should be just firm enough to gather into a ball. If necessary, add remaining ½ cup flour gradually, stirring until all flour is absorbed.)

Turn dough onto heavily floured surface; knead until smooth and elastic, about 10 minutes. Place in greased bowl; turn greased side up. Cover; let rise in warm place until dough is double, about 1½ hours. (Dough is ready if an indentation remains when touched lightly.)

Punch down dough; divide in half. Shape each half into a round, slightly flat loaf. Do not tear dough. Place loaves in opposite corners of greased baking sheet. Make three ¼-inch slashes in each loaf. Let rise until double, about 45 minutes.

Heat oven to 375°. Brush loaves with cold water. Place in middle of oven. Bake until loaves sound hollow when tapped, about 50 minutes, brushing occasionally with water. Remove from baking sheet; cool on wire racks.   2 LOAVES.

*Do not use self-rising flour in this recipe.

SOURDOUGH STARTER

1 teaspoon active dry yeast
¼ cup warm water (105 to 115°)
¾ cup milk
1 cup all-purpose flour*

Dissolve yeast in warm water in 3-quart glass bowl. Stir in milk. Stir in flour gradually. Beat until smooth. Cover with towel or cheesecloth; let stand in warm, draft-free place (80 to 85°) until starter begins to ferment, about 24 hours (bubbles will appear on surface of starter). If starter has not begun fermentation after 24 hours, discard and begin again. If fermentation has begun, stir well; cover tightly with plastic wrap and return to warm, draft-free place. Let starter stand until foamy, 2 to 3 days.

When starter has become foamy, stir well; pour into 1-quart crock or glass jar with tight fitting cover. Store in refrigerator. Starter is ready to use when a clear liquid has risen to top. Stir before using. Use 1 cup starter in recipe; reserve remaining starter. To remaining starter, add ¾ cup milk and ¾ cup flour. Store covered at room temperature until bubbles appear, about 12 hours; refrigerate.

Use starter regularly, every week or so. If the volume of the breads you bake begins to decrease, dissolve 1 teaspoon active dry yeast in ¼ cup warm water. Stir in ½ cup milk, ¾ cup flour and the remaining starter.

*Do not use self-rising flour in this recipe.

POTATO DOUGHNUTS

1 package active dry yeast
1½ cups warm water (105 to
    115°)
⅔ cup sugar
1½ teaspoons salt
⅔ cup shortening

2 eggs
1 cup lukewarm mashed
    cooked potatoes
6 to 7 cups all-purpose flour*
Glaze (below)

Dissolve yeast in warm water in 3-quart bowl. Stir in sugar, salt, shortening, eggs, potatoes and 3 cups of the flour. Beat until smooth. Mix in enough remaining flour to make dough easy to handle.

Turn dough onto well-floured surface; knead until smooth and elastic, about 5 minutes. Place in greased bowl; turn greased side up. Cover tightly; refrigerate at least 8 hours.

Punch down dough. Pat ¾ inch thick on lightly floured surface. Cut with floured 2½-inch doughnut cutter. Cover; let rise in warm place until indentation remains when touched, 45 to 60 minutes.

Heat vegetable oil or shortening (3 to 4 inches) to 375° in deep fat fryer or heavy saucepan. Fry doughnuts, turning once, until golden brown, 2 to 4 minutes; drain on paper. While warm, dip doughnuts in Glaze.   ABOUT 2½ DOZEN DOUGHNUTS.

*If using self-rising flour, omit salt.

GLAZE
Mix 3 cups powdered sugar and ½ cup boiling water until smooth.

BAKED GRITS WITH GARLIC CHEESE

2 cups milk
2 cups water
1 cup quick grits
1 teaspoon salt
¼ teaspoon pepper
1 package (6 ounces)
    garlic-flavored pasteurized
    process cheese spread

2 eggs, slightly beaten
1 tablespoon butter or
    margarine

Heat oven to 350°. Mix milk, water, grits, salt and pepper in 2-quart saucepan. Heat to boiling, stirring occasionally; reduce heat. Simmer uncovered, stirring frequently, until thick, about 5 minutes. Blend in cheese spread. Stir ¼ of the hot mixture into eggs; stir into remaining hot mixture in saucepan. Pour into greased 1½-quart casserole. Dot with butter. Bake uncovered 40 minutes. 6 TO 8 SERVINGS.

Pictured opposite.
A legacy of caring: Potato Doughnuts—and their holes—still warm and delicately glazed. Perhaps even better than those Great-grandma used to make!

Sticky buns, honey buns, pecan rolls—whatever they're called in your part of the country, these gooey-rich sweet rolls are an anytime natural with coffee, tea or milk.

STICKY BUNS

1 package active dry yeast
¼ cup warm water (105 to 115°)
¾ cup lukewarm milk (scalded, then cooled)
¼ cup granulated sugar
1 teaspoon salt
1 egg
½ cup butter or margarine, softened

3 to 3½ cups all-purpose flour*
Caramel Sauce (below)
1½ to 2 cups pecan halves
¼ cup butter or margarine, softened
½ cup granulated sugar
½ cup packed brown sugar
1½ teaspoons ground cinnamon

Dissolve yeast in warm water in 3-quart bowl. Stir in milk, ¼ cup granulated sugar, the salt, egg, ½ cup butter and 1½ cups of the flour. Beat until smooth. Mix in enough remaining flour to make dough easy to handle.

Turn dough onto lightly floured surface; knead until smooth and elastic, about 5 minutes. Place in greased bowl; turn greased side up. Cover; let rise in warm place until double, about 1½ hours. (Dough is ready if an indentation remains when touched.)

Pour about 1 tablespoon Caramel Sauce into each of 36 greased medium muffin cups (2¾ inches in diameter). Place 3 or 4 pecan halves flat sides up in sauce in each muffin cup.

Punch down dough; divide in half. Roll each half into rectangle, 18x9 inches, on lightly floured surface. Spread with 2 tablespoons butter. Mix ½ cup granulated sugar, the brown sugar and cinnamon. Sprinkle half of the sugar-cinnamon mixture evenly over each rectangle. Roll up tightly, beginning at one of the long sides. Pinch edge of dough into roll to seal. Stretch and shape until even. Cut each roll into 18 slices about 1 inch wide. Place 1 slice cut side down in each muffin cup. Let rise until double, about 45 minutes.

Heat oven to 375°. Bake until golden brown, 15 to 20 minutes. Immediately invert on large trays or baking sheets. Let pans remain a minute so caramel will drizzle down.   3 DOZEN BUNS.

*If using self-rising flour, omit salt.

CARAMEL SAUCE
Heat 1 cup packed brown sugar, 1 cup dark corn syrup and ¼ cup butter or margarine to boiling; reduce heat. Simmer uncovered 1 minute; cool.

SUNSHINE CAKE

8 egg whites
½ teaspoon cream of tartar
½ teaspoon salt
1½ cups sugar
5 egg yolks

1 cup all-purpose flour*
2 tablespoons water
½ teaspoon almond extract
½ teaspoon lemon extract
½ teaspoon vanilla

Heat oven to 325°. Beat egg whites, cream of tartar and salt in large mixer bowl until foamy. Beat in 1 cup of the sugar, 1 tablespoon at a time; continue beating until stiff and glossy. Reserve meringue.

Beat egg yolks in small mixer bowl until very thick and lemon colored, about 5 minutes. Beat in remaining ½ cup sugar gradually. Beat in flour alternately with water and flavorings on low speed. Fold egg yolk mixture into reserved meringue. Spread in ungreased tube pan, 10x4 inches. Cut through batter gently with spatula.

Bake until top springs back when touched lightly in center, 1 hour to 1 hour 5 minutes. Immediately invert pan on funnel; let hang until completely cool.

*If using self-rising flour, omit salt.

It seems that pound cakes, with their virtues of lasting well and not requiring a frosting, have always been a teatime standby. Old recipes call for a pound each of flour, eggs, butter and sugar, mixed and then baked in one-pound loaves. Here's an updated version that keeps the name but skips the pounds.

POUND CAKE

2¾ cups sugar
1¼ cups butter or margarine,
     softened
5 eggs
1 teaspoon vanilla

3 cups all-purpose flour*
1 teaspoon baking powder
½ teaspoon ground mace
¼ teaspoon salt
1 cup evaporated milk

Heat oven to 350°. Grease and flour tube pan, 10x4 inches, or 12-cup bundt cake pan. Beat sugar, butter, eggs and vanilla 30 seconds on low speed in large mixer bowl, scraping bowl constantly. Beat 5 minutes on high speed, scraping bowl occasionally. Beat in flour, baking powder, mace and salt alternately with milk on low speed. Spread in pan.

Bake until wooden pick inserted in center comes out clean, 1 hour 10 minutes to 1 hour 20 minutes. Cool 20 minutes; remove from pan. Cool completely.

*Do not use self-rising flour in this recipe.

HARD TIMES CAKE

1 cup packed brown sugar
2 teaspoons ground cinnamon
½ teaspoon ground nutmeg
½ teaspoon ground cloves
1¼ cups water
⅓ cup shortening

2 cups raisins
2 cups all-purpose flour*
1 teaspoon baking powder
1 teaspoon baking soda
1 teaspoon salt

Mix sugar, cinnamon, nutmeg, cloves, water, shortening and raisins in 2-quart saucepan. Heat to boiling. Boil uncovered 3 minutes; cool.

Heat oven to 325°. Grease and flour loaf pan, 9x5x3 inches, or baking pan, 9x9x2 inches. Mix flour, baking powder, baking soda and salt. Stir into raisin mixture. Pour into pan.

Bake until wooden pick inserted in center comes out clean, loaf about 1¼ hours, square about 55 minutes. Cool 10 minutes; remove from pan. Cool completely.

*Do not use self-rising flour in this recipe.

Of all the cakes baked in America, probably none are more loved than the chocolate ones. German Chocolate Cake and Midwest Chocolate Cake are two of the finest. A version of German Chocolate was brought to Texas in the early 1800s, and below is the grass-roots recipe that swept the country to become a classic. Midwest Chocolate Cake is a down-home favorite that is as rich as chocolate can be.

GERMAN CHOCOLATE CAKE

½ cup boiling water
1 bar (4 ounces) sweet cooking
   chocolate
2 cups sugar
1 cup butter or margarine,
   softened
4 egg yolks
1 teaspoon vanilla

2½ cups cake flour
1 teaspoon baking soda
1 teaspoon salt
1 cup buttermilk
4 egg whites, stiffly beaten
Coconut-Pecan Frosting
   (page 23)

Heat oven to 350°. Grease 3 round layer pans, 8 or 9x1½ inches, or 2 baking pans, 8x8x2 or 9x9x2 inches. Line bottoms of pans with waxed paper. Pour boiling water over chocolate, stirring until chocolate is melted; cool.

Beat sugar and butter in large mixer bowl until light and fluffy. Beat in egg yolks, 1 at a time. Blend in chocolate and vanilla on low speed. Mix in flour, baking soda and salt alternately with buttermilk; continue beating after each addition until batter is smooth. Fold in egg whites. Divide among pans.

Bake until top springs back when touched lightly in center, 8-inch rounds 35 to 40 minutes, 9-inch rounds 30 to 35 minutes, 8-inch squares 45 to 50 minutes, 9-inch squares 40 to 45 minutes. Cool 10 minutes; remove from pans. Cool completely. Fill layers and frost top of cake with Coconut-Pecan Frosting.

COCONUT-PECAN FROSTING

1 cup sugar
1 cup evaporated milk
½ cup butter or margarine
3 egg yolks

1 teaspoon vanilla
1⅓ cups flaked coconut
1 cup chopped pecans

Mix sugar, milk, butter, egg yolks and vanilla in 1-quart saucepan. Cook over medium heat, stirring frequently, until thick, about 12 minutes. Remove from heat; stir in coconut and pecans. Beat until of spreading consistency.

MIDWEST CHOCOLATE CAKE

2 cups all-purpose flour*
2 cups sugar
1 cup water
¾ cup dairy sour cream
¼ cup shortening
1¼ teaspoons baking soda
1 teaspoon salt

½ teaspoon baking powder
2 eggs
1 teaspoon vanilla
4 ounces melted unsweetened
   chocolate (cool)
Chocolaty Chocolate Frosting
   (below)

Heat oven to 350°. Grease and flour two 9-inch or three 8-inch round layer pans. Beat all ingredients except frosting 30 seconds on low speed in large mixer bowl, scraping bowl constantly. Beat 3 minutes on high speed, scraping bowl occasionally. Pour into pans.

Bake until top springs back when touched lightly in center, 30 to 35 minutes. Cool 10 minutes; remove from pans. Cool completely. Fill layers and frost cake with Chocolaty Chocolate Frosting; refrigerate.

*If using self-rising flour, reduce baking soda to ¼ teaspoon, omit salt and baking powder.

CHOCOLATY CHOCOLATE FROSTING

5 ounces melted unsweetened
   chocolate (cool)
2½ cups powdered sugar
¼ cup hot water

4 egg yolks
⅓ cup butter or margarine,
   softened

Mix chocolate, 1½ cups of the sugar and the hot water until smooth; stir in remaining sugar. Beat in egg yolks, 1 at a time, until smooth. Beat in butter.

A cake from the grand tradition —just as perfect for a conclusion to a holiday feast now as it was when it waited on the polished sideboards of colonial Williamsburg or bluegrass Kentucky.

Whenever a recipe begins with caramelized sugar, you can be sure of a sumptuous sweetness. Our Burnt Sugar Cake is further endowed with a delicious Caramel Frosting.

BURNT SUGAR CAKE

1½ cups sugar	2¼ cups all-purpose flour*
½ cup boiling water	3 teaspoons baking powder
2 eggs, separated	1 teaspoon salt
½ cup butter or margarine, softened	1 cup milk
1 teaspoon vanilla	Caramel Frosting (below)

Heat ½ cup of the sugar in heavy 8-inch skillet, stirring constantly, until sugar is melted and golden brown. Remove from heat; stir in boiling water slowly. Cook over low heat, stirring constantly, until sugar lumps are dissolved. Add enough water to syrup, if necessary, to measure ½ cup; cool.

Heat oven to 375°. Grease and flour two 9-inch or three 8-inch round layer pans. Beat egg whites in small mixer bowl until foamy. Beat in ½ cup of the sugar, 1 tablespoon at a time; continue beating until very stiff and glossy. Reserve meringue.

Beat butter, remaining ½ cup sugar, the egg yolks and vanilla 30 seconds on low speed in large mixer bowl, scraping bowl constantly. Beat 5 minutes on high speed, scraping bowl occasionally. Beat in syrup. Beat in flour, baking powder and salt alternately with milk. Fold in reserved meringue. Pour into pans.

Bake until wooden pick inserted in center comes out clean, 20 to 25 minutes. Cool 10 minutes; remove from pans. Cool completely. Fill layers and frost cake with Caramel Frosting. Arrange pecan or walnut halves around top edge of cake if desired.

*If using self-rising flour, omit baking powder and salt.

CARAMEL FROSTING

2 tablespoons butter or margarine	⅓ cup whipping cream or evaporated milk
⅔ cup packed dark brown sugar	2⅓ to 2½ cups powdered sugar
⅛ teaspoon salt	½ teaspoon vanilla

Heat butter in 2-quart saucepan until melted. Stir in brown sugar, salt and cream. Heat to boiling, stirring constantly. Remove from heat; cool to lukewarm. Stir in enough powdered sugar gradually until of spreading consistency. Stir in vanilla.

Pictured opposite.
Burnt Sugar Cake with Caramel Frosting—a flavorful cake from yesterday, every bit as delicious today.

LANE CAKE

8 egg whites
2 cups sugar
1 cup butter or margarine,
  softened
1 teaspoon vanilla

3¼ cups all-purpose flour*
3½ teaspoons baking powder
¾ teaspoon salt
1 cup milk
Lane Frosting (below)

Heat oven to 350°. Grease and flour 2 round layer pans, 9x1½ inches. Beat egg whites in large mixer bowl until foamy. Beat in 1 cup of the sugar, 1 tablespoon at a time; continue beating until stiff and glossy. Reserve meringue.

Beat remaining 1 cup sugar, the butter and vanilla 30 seconds on low speed in large mixer bowl, scraping bowl constantly. Beat 5 minutes on high speed, scraping bowl occasionally. Beat in flour, baking powder and salt alternately with milk (batter will be stiff). Stir ¼ of the reserved meringue into flour mixture. Fold in remaining meringue. Spread about 2 cups evenly in each pan. Refrigerate remaining batter.

Bake until wooden pick inserted in center comes out clean, 25 to 30 minutes. Cool 10 minutes; remove from pans. Repeat with remaining batter; cool. Fill layers and frost top of cake with Lane Frosting, allowing some to drizzle down side. To store cake, wrap in plastic wrap or aluminum foil and refrigerate. Cake can be refrigerated up to 3 weeks or frozen up to 2 months (flavor mellows with storage).   20 SERVINGS.

*If using self-rising flour, omit baking powder and salt.

NOTE: All the batter can be baked at once in 2 round layer pans, 9x1½ inches, 40 to 45 minutes. Cool; split layers horizontally in half.

LANE FROSTING

¾ cup butter or margarine
12 egg yolks, slightly beaten
2 cups minus 2 tablespoons
  sugar
¾ teaspoon salt
1½ cups chopped pecans

1½ cups chopped raisins
1½ cups shredded coconut
1½ cups red candied cherries,
  cut into fourths
⅓ cup bourbon

Heat butter in 3-quart saucepan over low heat until melted. Stir in egg yolks, sugar and salt. Cook over low heat, stirring constantly, until mixture is slightly thickened, about 10 minutes (do not boil). Remove from heat; stir in remaining ingredients. Cool. If necessary, stir in additional bourbon until of spreading consistency.

NOTE: Leftover egg whites can be refrigerated up to 10 days in tightly covered container, or they can be frozen.

LADY BALTIMORE CAKE

½ cup raisins, chopped
6 dried figs, cut up
3 tablespoons cognac or brandy
½ cup chopped pecans

Seven-Minute Frosting (below)
8- or 9-inch two-layer white
 cake

Mix raisins, figs and cognac; let stand until cognac is absorbed, about 1 hour. Stir in pecans. Stir raisin mixture into 1 cup of the frosting; fill layers. Frost cake with remaining frosting.

SEVEN-MINUTE FROSTING

1½ cups sugar
¼ teaspoon cream of tartar or 1
 tablespoon light corn syrup

⅓ cup water
2 egg whites
1 teaspoon vanilla

Mix sugar, cream of tartar, water and egg whites in top of double boiler. Beat 1 minute on high speed. Place over boiling water (water should not touch bottom of pan). Beat 7 minutes on high speed. Remove pan from water; add vanilla. Beat 2 minutes on high speed.

OLD-FASHIONED FRUITCAKE

3 cups all-purpose flour*
1⅓ cups sugar
2 teaspoons salt
1 teaspoon baking powder
2 teaspoons ground cinnamon
1 teaspoon ground nutmeg
1 cup orange juice
1 cup vegetable oil
¼ cup dark corn syrup

4 eggs
2 cups raisins
1 pound mixed candied fruits
 (2 cups)
1 package (8 ounces) pitted
 dates, cut up (1½ cups)
½ pound pecan halves (about 2
 cups)

Heat oven to 275°. Line 2 loaf pans, 9x5x3 or 8½x4½x2½ inches, with aluminum foil; grease. Beat all ingredients except fruits and nuts 30 seconds on low speed in large mixer bowl, scraping bowl constantly. Beat 3 minutes on high speed, scraping bowl occasionally. Stir in fruits and nuts. Spread evenly in pans.

Bake until wooden pick inserted in center comes out clean, 2½ to 3 hours. Cover with aluminum foil during last hour of baking, if necessary, to prevent excessive browning. Remove from pans; cool. Wrap in plastic wrap or aluminum foil and store in refrigerator or cool place.

*Do not use self-rising flour in this recipe.

NOTE: Best made 3 or 4 weeks in advance. Can be wrapped in wine- or brandy-dampened cloth.

YELLOW FRUITCAKE

3 cups all-purpose flour*
1½ cups sugar
1½ teaspoons baking powder
¾ teaspoon salt
¾ cup shortening
¾ cup butter or margarine,
    softened
⅔ cup orange juice
9 eggs
1 package (15 ounces) golden
    raisins (about 3 cups)
1 pound candied cherries, cut
    in halves (about 2½ cups)

¾ pound candied pineapple,
    cut up (about 2 cups)
¼ pound candied citron, cut up
    (about ⅔ cup)
¼ pound candied orange peel,
    cut up (about ⅔ cup)
½ pound pecan halves (about 2
    cups)
½ pound blanched whole
    almonds (1½ cups)
1 can (3½ ounces) flaked
    coconut

Heat oven to 275°. Line 2 loaf pans, 9x5x3 inches, with aluminum foil; grease. Beat all ingredients except fruits and nuts 30 seconds on low speed in large mixer bowl, scraping bowl constantly. Beat 3 minutes on high speed, scraping bowl occasionally. Stir in fruits and nuts. Spread evenly in pans.

Bake until wooden pick inserted in center comes out clean, 2½ to 3 hours. Cover with aluminum foil during last hour of baking, if necessary, to prevent excessive browning. Remove from pans; cool. Wrap in plastic wrap or aluminum foil and store in refrigerator or cool place.

*Do not use self-rising flour in this recipe.

SNOWBALLS

1 cup all-purpose flour*
¾ cup sugar
1¾ teaspoons baking powder
½ teaspoon salt
½ cup milk
¼ cup shortening

½ teaspoon vanilla
2 egg whites
Sweetened whipped cream
Crushed sweetened peaches or
    strawberries

Grease eight 6-ounce custard cups generously. Beat all ingredients except egg whites, whipped cream and peaches 30 seconds on low speed in small mixer bowl, scraping bowl constantly. Beat 1 minute on high speed, scraping bowl occasionally. Add egg whites; beat 2 minutes on high speed, scraping bowl occasionally. Pour into custard cups, filling each about ½ full. Cover each loosely with aluminum foil.

Place custard cups on rack in Dutch oven or roasting pan; pour boiling water into pan to depth of 1½ inches. Cover pan. Keep water boiling over low heat until wooden pick inserted in center of cake comes out clean, about 40 minutes.

Remove custard cups from pan and let stand 10 minutes; unmold. Serve warm with whipped cream and peaches.   8 CAKES.

*Do not use self-rising flour in this recipe.

Coconut Snowballs: Cool cakes. Prepare your favorite fluffy white frosting. Roll each cake in frosting, using 2 spoons to turn; smooth off excess frosting with knife. Place on dessert plates and sprinkle generously with grated or shredded coconut. Serve with chocolate, caramel or strawberry sauce if desired.

NOTE: If all cups do not fit in pan, steam as many as possible; refrigerate others and steam later.

PINEAPPLE UPSIDE-DOWN CAKE

¼ cup butter or margarine
1 can (20 ounces) sliced
   pineapple in heavy syrup
⅔ cup packed brown sugar
Maraschino cherries (optional)
1½ cups cake flour or 1¼ cups
   all-purpose flour*
1 cup granulated sugar

1½ teaspoons baking powder
½ teaspoon salt
¾ cup milk
⅓ cup shortening
1 egg
1 teaspoon vanilla
Sweetened whipped cream

Heat oven to 350°. Heat butter in oven in 9-inch ovenproof skillet or baking pan, 9x9x2 inches, until melted. Drain pineapple, reserving 2 tablespoons syrup. Stir syrup into butter; sprinkle evenly with brown sugar. Arrange pineapple slices in butter mixture. Place cherry in center of each pineapple slice.

Beat remaining ingredients except cream 30 seconds on low speed in large mixer bowl, scraping bowl constantly. Beat 3 minutes on high speed, scraping bowl occasionally. Pour evenly over pineapple slices.

Bake until wooden pick inserted in center comes out clean, 40 to 45 minutes. Invert on heatproof platter. Leave skillet over cake a few minutes. Serve warm with whipped cream.   9 SERVINGS.

*If using self-rising flour, omit baking powder and salt.

Apricot Upside-down Cake: Substitute 1 can (about 17 ounces) apricot halves for the pineapple slices.

Peach Upside-down Cake: Substitute 1 can (about 16 ounces) sliced peaches for the pineapple slices.

Plum Upside-down Cake: Substitute 1 can (about 17 ounces) Greengage or purple plums, cut in halves and pitted, for the pineapple slices.

MAPLE-NUT CHIFFON CAKE

2 cups all-purpose flour*
¾ cup granulated sugar
¾ cup packed brown sugar
3 teaspoons baking powder
1 teaspoon salt
½ cup vegetable oil
7 egg yolks

¾ cup cold water
2 teaspoons maple flavoring
1 cup egg whites (7 or 8)
½ teaspoon cream of tartar
1 cup very finely chopped nuts
Browned Butter Glaze (below)

Heat oven to 325°. Mix flour, granulated sugar, brown sugar, baking powder and salt. Make a "well" and add in order: oil, egg yolks, water and maple flavoring. Beat with spoon until smooth. Beat egg whites and cream of tartar in large mixer bowl until stiff peaks form. Pour egg yolk mixture gradually over egg whites, folding just until blended. Sprinkle nuts over batter; fold in with a few strokes. Pour into ungreased tube pan, 10x4 inches. Cut through batter gently with spatula.

Bake until top springs back when touched lightly in center, 60 to 70 minutes. Immediately invert pan on funnel; let hang until completely cool. Spread cake with Browned Butter Glaze, allowing some to drizzle down side.

*If using self-rising flour, omit baking powder and salt.

BROWNED BUTTER GLAZE

⅓ cup butter
2 cups powdered sugar

1½ teaspoons vanilla
2 to 4 tablespoons hot water

Heat butter in 2-quart saucepan over medium heat until light brown; cool slightly. Blend in sugar and vanilla. Stir in water, 1 tablespoon at a time, until of spreading consistency.

HOT WATER SPONGE CAKE

3 eggs
¾ cup sugar
⅓ cup hot water or hot milk
1 teaspoon vanilla

½ teaspoon lemon extract
1¼ cups cake flour
1½ teaspoons baking powder
½ teaspoon salt

Heat oven to 350°. Grease and flour baking pan, 8x8x2 or 9x9x2 inches. Beat eggs in small mixer bowl on high speed 5 minutes; pour into large mixer bowl. Beat in sugar gradually. Beat in water, vanilla and lemon extract on low speed. Beat in flour, baking powder and salt on low speed; continue beating just until batter is smooth. Pour into pan.

Bake until top springs back when touched lightly in center, 25 to 30 minutes; cool. Nice served with sweetened sliced strawberries.

Pictured opposite.
A delectable demonstration of the versatility of nuts. From top: Maple-Nut Chiffon Cake (this page), Pecan Pie (page 47) and Filbert Bars (page 40).

Not a true pie, not quite a cake or custard, Boston Cream Pie has good qualities from each. Martha Washington's version is said to have had jam, and sometimes cream filling, sandwiched between layers with powdered sugar sprinkled on top, but Americans have long since opted for custard and chocolate.

Boston Cream Pie is always a pleasing combination of textures and subtle flavors. Because of the custard filling, this pie must be stored in the refrigerator.

BOSTON CREAM PIE

1½ cups cake flour or 1¼ cups
   all-purpose flour*
1 cup sugar
1½ teaspoons baking powder
½ teaspoon salt
¾ cup milk

⅓ cup shortening
1 egg
1 teaspoon vanilla
Cream Filling (below)
Chocolate Glaze (below)

Heat oven to 350°. Grease and flour round layer pan, 9x1½ inches. Beat all ingredients except filling and glaze 30 seconds on low speed in large mixer bowl, scraping bowl constantly. Beat 3 minutes on high speed, scraping bowl occasionally. Pour into pan.

Bake until wooden pick inserted in center comes out clean, about 35 minutes. Cool 10 minutes; remove from pan. Cool completely. Split cake horizontally in half. Fill layers with Cream Filling. Spread top of cake with Chocolate Glaze; refrigerate.

*If using self-rising flour, omit baking powder and salt.

CREAM FILLING
⅓ cup sugar
2 tablespoons cornstarch
⅛ teaspoon salt

1½ cups milk
2 egg yolks, slightly beaten
2 teaspoons vanilla

Mix sugar, cornstarch and salt in 2-quart saucepan. Mix milk and egg yolks; stir gradually into sugar mixture. Cook over medium heat, stirring constantly, until mixture thickens and boils. Boil and stir 1 minute. Remove from heat. Stir in vanilla; cool.

CHOCOLATE GLAZE
3 tablespoons butter or
   margarine
2 squares (1 ounce each)
   unsweetened chocolate

1 cup powdered sugar
¾ teaspoon vanilla
About 2 tablespoons hot water

Heat butter and chocolate in 1-quart saucepan over low heat, stirring constantly, until chocolate is melted. Remove from heat; stir in sugar and vanilla. Stir in water, 1 teaspoon at a time, until smooth and of spreading consistency.

ORANGE-LEMON REFRIGERATOR CAKE

1 cup plus 2 tablespoons
   all-purpose flour*
1 cup granulated sugar
2 teaspoons baking powder
¾ teaspoon salt
½ cup cold water
⅓ cup vegetable oil

3 egg yolks
5 or 6 egg whites (⅔ cup)
½ teaspoon cream of tartar
Orange-Lemon Filling (below)
1 cup chilled whipping cream
¼ cup powdered sugar

Heat oven to 350°. Mix flour, granulated sugar, baking powder and salt. Stir in water, oil and egg yolks until smooth. Beat egg whites and cream of tartar in large mixer bowl until stiff peaks form. Pour egg yolk mixture gradually over egg whites, folding just until blended. Pour into 2 ungreased round layer pans, 8 or 9x1½ inches.

Bake until top springs back when touched lightly in center, 30 to 35 minutes. Immediately invert pans with edges on 2 other pans; let hang until layers are completely cool. Loosen edges from pans with spatula. Turn pans over; hit edges sharply to loosen completely.

Split cake layers horizontally in half. Stack layers, spreading ½ cup of the Orange-Lemon Filling between layers. Frost top and side of cake with remaining filling. Wrap in plastic wrap or aluminum foil and refrigerate at least 12 hours.

Just before serving, beat whipping cream and powdered sugar in chilled bowl until stiff; frost cake. Garnish with grated orange or lemon peel if desired; refrigerate.

*If using self-rising flour, omit baking powder and salt.

ORANGE-LEMON FILLING

½ cup sugar
2 tablespoons cornstarch
⅛ teaspoon salt
1 cup orange juice
½ cup water
2 egg yolks, slightly beaten
2 tablespoons lemon juice

1 tablespoon grated orange
   peel
1 tablespoon butter or
   margarine
2 egg whites
¼ cup sugar

Mix ½ cup sugar, the cornstarch and salt in 2-quart saucepan. Stir in orange juice and water gradually. Cook over medium heat, stirring constantly, until mixture thickens and boils. Boil and stir 1 minute. Stir at least half of the hot mixture slowly into egg yolks. Blend egg yolk mixture into hot mixture in saucepan. Boil 1 minute, stirring constantly. Remove from heat. Stir in juice, peel and butter; cool.

Beat egg whites until foamy. Beat in ¼ cup sugar, 1 tablespoon at a time; continue beating until stiff and glossy. Fold orange mixture into egg whites.

COOKIES

A special treat for good girls and boys always has been, and still is, cookies. Hermits, Joe Froggers, Jumbles and Chocolate Crinkles come from a long line of cookies with whimsical names. There were Petticoat Tails, Snickerdoodles, Brambles, Tangle Breeches, Wasps' Nests—names that give away the nature of all these cookies, which is that they're for fun, both to say and to eat.

HERMITS

2 cups packed brown sugar
1 teaspoon baking soda
1 teaspoon salt
1 teaspoon ground cinnamon
1 teaspoon ground nutmeg
½ cup shortening
½ cup butter or margarine, softened

½ cup cold coffee
2 eggs
3½ cups all-purpose flour*
2½ cups raisins
1½ cups chopped nuts

Heat oven to 375°. Mix sugar, baking soda, salt, cinnamon, nutmeg, shortening, butter, coffee and eggs. Stir in flour, raisins and nuts. Drop dough by rounded teaspoonfuls 2 inches apart onto ungreased baking sheet.

Bake until almost no imprint remains when touched lightly in center, 8 to 10 minutes.   ABOUT 8 DOZEN COOKIES.

*If using self-rising flour, omit baking soda and salt.

SOFT PUMPKIN COOKIES

1 cup sugar
1 cup canned pumpkin
½ cup shortening
1 tablespoon grated orange peel
2 cups all-purpose flour*
1 teaspoon baking powder

1 teaspoon baking soda
1 teaspoon ground cinnamon
¼ teaspoon salt
½ cup raisins
½ cup chopped nuts

Heat oven to 375°. Mix sugar, pumpkin, shortening and orange peel. Stir in flour, baking powder, baking soda, cinnamon and salt. Stir in raisins and nuts. Drop dough by teaspoonfuls onto ungreased baking sheet. Bake until light brown, 8 to 10 minutes.   ABOUT 4 DOZEN COOKIES.

*If using self-rising flour, omit baking powder, baking soda and salt.

Chocolate Chip-Pumpkin Cookies: Substitute ½ cup semisweet chocolate chips for the raisins or nuts.

Known as sesame seeds in most of the country, "benne" is the name Southerners learned to call these seeds, which were brought from Africa by slaves. Toasting benne seeds develops their flavor and also gives these cookies a slightly crunchy texture.

BENNE SEED COOKIES

1 cup benne (sesame) seed
1½ cups packed brown sugar
1 cup all-purpose flour*
¼ teaspoon baking powder
¼ teaspoon salt

¾ cup butter or margarine, melted
1 egg
1 teaspoon vanilla

Heat oven to 375°. Toast benne seed on ungreased baking sheet until brown, 10 to 12 minutes. Mix all ingredients. Drop dough by ½ teaspoonfuls 1½ inches apart onto greased baking sheet.

Bake until brown, 4 to 6 minutes. Cool about 30 seconds before removing from baking sheet.   ABOUT 6 DOZEN COOKIES.

*If using self-rising flour, omit baking powder and salt.

JUMBLES

2¾ cups all-purpose flour*
1½ cups packed brown sugar
1 teaspoon salt
½ teaspoon baking soda
1 cup dairy sour cream

½ cup shortening
2 eggs
1 teaspoon vanilla
1 cup chopped nuts (optional)
Browned Butter Glaze (page 30)

Mix all ingredients except glaze. Cover and refrigerate if soft.

Heat oven to 375°. Drop dough by level tablespoonfuls 2 inches apart onto ungreased baking sheet.

Bake until almost no imprint remains when touched lightly in center, about 10 minutes. Immediately remove from baking sheet; cool. Spread with Browned Butter Glaze.   ABOUT 4½ DOZEN COOKIES.

*If using self-rising flour, omit salt and baking soda.

Applesauce Jumbles: Omit sour cream and stir in ¾ cup applesauce, 1 teaspoon ground cinnamon, ¼ teaspoon ground cloves and 1 cup raisins.

Fruit Jumbles: Omit nuts and stir in 2 cups candied cherries, cut in halves, 2 cups cut-up dates and 1½ cups chopped pecans. Drop dough by rounded teaspoonfuls onto ungreased baking sheet. Place a pecan half on each cookie. Omit glaze.   ABOUT 7 DOZEN COOKIES.

CHOCOLATE CRINKLES

½ cup vegetable oil
4 ounces melted unsweetened
   chocolate (cool)
2 cups granulated sugar
2 teaspoons vanilla

4 eggs
2 cups all-purpose flour*
2 teaspoons baking powder
½ teaspoon salt
1 cup powdered sugar

Mix oil, chocolate, granulated sugar and vanilla. Blend in eggs, 1 at a time. Stir in flour, baking powder and salt. Cover and refrigerate at least 3 hours.

Heat oven to 350°. Drop dough by teaspoonfuls into powdered sugar; roll in sugar. Shape into balls. Place about 2 inches apart on greased baking sheet. Bake until almost no imprint remains when touched lightly in center, 10 to 12 minutes.   ABOUT 6 DOZEN COOKIES.

*If using self-rising flour, omit baking powder and salt.

Ginger was one of the prize spices settlers could obtain from the ships that plied the West Indies. Among their earliest desserts were heavy ginger cakes sweetened with dark molasses. Later, German and Dutch settlers in New York and Pennsylvania baked light gingerbread, large cookies shaped like people and crisp gingersnaps. Virtually every generation of American children since has favored goodies spiced with ginger.

These spicy Gingersnaps and hot chocolate make a perfect welcome-home snack on a blustery day.

GINGERSNAPS

1 cup sugar
¾ cup shortening
¼ cup dark molasses
1 egg
2¼ cups all-purpose flour*

1½ teaspoons baking soda
1 tablespoon ground ginger
1 teaspoon ground cinnamon
¼ teaspoon salt
Sugar

Mix 1 cup sugar, the shortening, molasses and egg. Stir in remaining ingredients except sugar. Cover and refrigerate 1 hour.

Heat oven to 375°. Shape dough by rounded teaspoonfuls into balls; dip tops in sugar. Place sugared sides up 3 inches apart on lightly greased baking sheet.

Bake until edges of cookies are set (centers will be soft), 10 to 12 minutes. Immediately remove from baking sheet.   ABOUT 4 DOZEN COOKIES.

*If using self-rising flour, omit baking soda and salt.

FARM-STYLE OATMEAL COOKIES

2 cups packed brown sugar
1 cup lard or 1 cup plus 2
   tablespoons shortening,
   melted
½ cup buttermilk

1 teaspoon vanilla
4 cups quick-cooking oats
1¾ cups all-purpose flour*
1 teaspoon baking soda
¾ teaspoon salt

Heat oven to 375°. Mix sugar, lard, buttermilk and vanilla. Stir in remaining ingredients. Shape dough into 1-inch balls. Place 3 inches apart on ungreased baking sheet. Flatten cookies with glass dipped in water to 2½ inches in diameter.

Bake until golden brown, 8 to 10 minutes. Immediately remove from baking sheet. Store in tightly covered container. ABOUT 7 DOZEN COOKIES.

*If using self-rising flour, omit baking soda and salt.

REFRIGERATOR NUT COOKIES

1 cup sugar
1 cup butter or margarine,
   softened
2 eggs
1½ teaspoons vanilla

3 cups all-purpose flour*
1 teaspoon salt
½ teaspoon baking soda
½ cup finely chopped nuts

Mix sugar, butter, eggs and vanilla. Stir in flour, salt, baking soda and nuts. Divide dough into 3 parts. Shape each part into roll 1½ inches in diameter and about 7 inches long. Wrap in waxed paper or plastic wrap and refrigerate at least 4 hours.

Heat oven to 400°. Cut dough into ⅛-inch slices. Place 1 inch apart on ungreased baking sheet.

Bake until light brown, 8 to 10 minutes. Immediately remove from baking sheet.   ABOUT 7 DOZEN COOKIES.

*If using self-rising flour, omit salt.

Butterscotch Slices: Substitute 1 cup packed brown sugar for the sugar; omit nuts.

Cinnamon Slices: Substitute ½ cup granulated sugar and ½ cup packed brown sugar for the sugar and 1 tablespoon ground cinnamon for the vanilla; omit nuts.

Orange-Almond Slices: Stir in 1 tablespoon grated orange peel with the sugar and substitute ½ cup finely chopped blanched almonds for the nuts.

America's settlers prepared all their meals in kitchens like this one at the Pilgrim Village restoration in Plymouth, Massachusetts.

Sour cream adds a special touch to many foods, including these delicious cookies. And nowadays you don't sour your own cream, as your ancestors did.

OLD-FASHIONED SOUR CREAM COOKIES

1 cup sugar
¼ cup shortening
¼ cup butter or margarine,
   softened
1 egg
1 teaspoon vanilla
2⅔ cups all-purpose flour*

1 teaspoon baking powder
½ teaspoon baking soda
½ teaspoon salt
¼ teaspoon ground nutmeg
½ cup dairy sour cream
Sugar

Heat oven to 425°. Mix 1 cup sugar, the shortening, butter, egg and vanilla. Stir in remaining ingredients except sugar. Divide dough into 3 parts. Roll each part ¼ inch thick on lightly floured cloth-covered board. Cut with 2-inch cookie cutter; sprinkle with sugar. Place on ungreased baking sheet.

Bake until almost no imprint remains when touched lightly in center, 6 to 8 minutes. ABOUT 4½ DOZEN COOKIES.

*If using self-rising flour, omit baking powder, baking soda and salt.

NOTE: Dough can be shaped by tablespoonfuls into balls, then flattened on baking sheet with greased bottom of glass dipped in sugar.

JOE FROGGERS

1 cup sugar
½ cup shortening
1 cup dark molasses
½ cup water
4 cups all-purpose flour*
1½ teaspoons salt

1 teaspoon baking soda
1½ teaspoons ground ginger
½ teaspoon ground cloves
½ teaspoon ground nutmeg
¼ teaspoon ground allspice
Sugar

Mix 1 cup sugar and the shortening. Stir in remaining ingredients except sugar. Cover and refrigerate at least 3 hours.

Heat oven to 375°. Roll dough ¼ inch thick on lightly floured cloth-covered board. Cut into 3-inch circles; sprinkle with sugar. Place on well-greased baking sheet.

Bake until almost no imprint remains when touched lightly in center, 10 to 12 minutes. Cool about 2 minutes before removing from baking sheet. ABOUT 3½ DOZEN COOKIES.

*If using self-rising flour, omit salt and baking soda.

Pictured opposite.
Milk and cookies—then as now, the perfect anytime treat: sugar-dusted Joe Froggers (bottom) and Old-fashioned Sour Cream Cookies (top).

FILLED DATE BARS

Date Filling (below)
1 cup packed brown sugar
½ cup butter or margarine,
   softened
¼ cup shortening

1¾ cups all-purpose flour*
1 teaspoon salt
½ teaspoon baking soda
1½ cups quick-cooking oats

Prepare Date Filling; cool.

Heat oven to 400°. Mix sugar, butter and shortening. Stir in remaining ingredients. Press half of the sugar mixture evenly in greased baking pan, 13x9x2 inches. Spread with filling. Sprinkle remaining sugar mixture over filling, pressing lightly.

Bake until light brown, 25 to 30 minutes. Cool slightly. Cut into bars, about 2x1½ inches.   3 DOZEN COOKIES.

*If using self-rising flour, omit salt and baking soda.

DATE FILLING
Mix 3 cups cut-up dates (1 pound), ¼ cup sugar and 1½ cups water. Cook over low heat, stirring constantly, until thickened, about 10 minutes.

Bar cookies weren't invented in America, but so many developed here that they have become an integral part of our baking heritage. The preeminent bar cookie is, of course, the brownie. More unusual are Filled Date Bars and Filbert Bars. A late variation on the many dried fruit bar cookies, Filled Date Bars became popular in the twentieth century when the California date crops began to flourish. Filberts, or hazelnuts, make a bar cookie with a nice crunch.

FILBERT BARS

1 cup sugar
1 cup butter or margarine,
   softened
1 egg, separated

1½ cups all-purpose flour*
¼ teaspoon salt
1 cup finely chopped filberts

Heat oven to 275°. Mix sugar, butter and egg yolk. Stir in flour and salt. Spread in ungreased jelly roll pan, 15½x10½x1 inch. Beat egg white slightly; brush over dough. Sprinkle filberts evenly over top, pressing lightly.

Bake until golden brown, about 1 hour. Immediately cut into bars, about 2x1 inch. Cool and store in tightly covered container. 75 COOKIES.

*If using self-rising flour, omit salt.

The American passion for chocolate started early and shows no signs of abating. Although chocolate originated in the Americas, it made a circuitous entrance into North American cooking. Explorers took cacao beans, from which chocolate is made, back to Spain from Mexico and South America, where the Indians used them extensively. It is said they even had their own version of an ice-cream drink: liquefied cacao poured over mountain snow.

When the English came to America, chocolate came back with them. By 1765 there already was a chocolate processing factory in New England. Americans were turning out cookies, cakes, pies and candies whenever they could afford chocolate and sugar. Hot chocolate became a favorite drink after the British tea tax was imposed. Later, when the cost of refining was reduced, chocolate was produced in quantity. The following recipe for Double-frosted Brownies is after the true chocolate-lover's heart.

DOUBLE-FROSTED BROWNIES

½ cup butter or margarine
2 squares (1 ounce each)
　　unsweetened chocolate
1 cup granulated sugar
2 eggs
1 teaspoon vanilla
½ cup all-purpose flour*
¼ teaspoon salt

½ cup chopped walnuts
1½ cups powdered sugar
½ cup whipping cream
⅓ cup butter or margarine
1 teaspoon vanilla
3 squares (1 ounce each)
　　unsweetened chocolate

Heat oven to 350°. Heat ½ cup butter and 2 squares chocolate in 2-quart saucepan over low heat, stirring constantly, until melted. Remove from heat; stir in granulated sugar, eggs and 1 teaspoon vanilla. Stir in flour, salt and walnuts. Spread dough in greased baking pan, 9x9x2 inches, or baking dish, 11¾x7½x1¾ inches.

Bake until brownies begin to pull away from sides of pan, 20 to 25 minutes; cool.

Heat powdered sugar, cream and ⅓ cup butter to boiling in 2-quart saucepan over medium heat, stirring constantly. Boil, without stirring, until candy thermometer registers 234° (or until small amount of mixture dropped into very cold water forms a soft ball that flattens when removed from water). Cool slightly. Beat in 1 teaspoon vanilla until smooth and of spreading consistency; spread topping over cooled brownies.

Heat 3 squares chocolate over low heat until melted; cool. Spread over topping. Refrigerate until chocolate is set. (Refrigerate until 1 hour before serving in warm weather.)　5 DOZEN COOKIES.

*If using self-rising flour, omit salt.

PIES

Pies were baked early in the morning on farms, and pie for breakfast seemed perfectly natural. Fresh Blueberry Tart and other glorious fruit pies swimming in bright juice were summer favorites, but winter brought out the pie baker's inventiveness with nuts, dried fruits and root vegetables such as carrots and sweet potatoes. At times even those were gone. This happened often enough to give the last weeks of winter the poignant name "the six weeks want." It must have been at such a time that someone with an intense taste for apple pie spotted the cider vinegar and, with true ingenuity, created Vinegar Pie, with its tart hint of apples.

Every farmhouse used to have a pie safe, a large cabinet with pierced tin or screened doors. Inside, safe from insects, cooled the day's pies. Modern pies, whether latticed, double crust or deep dish, use a flaky tried-and-true pastry like the one below.

PASTRY

8- OR 9-INCH ONE-CRUST PIE OR BAKED PIE SHELL
1 cup all-purpose flour*
½ teaspoon salt
⅓ cup plus 1 tablespoon shortening or ⅓ cup lard
2 to 3 tablespoons cold water

8- OR 9-INCH TWO-CRUST PIE
2 cups all-purpose flour*
1 teaspoon salt
⅔ cup plus 2 tablespoons shortening or ⅔ cup lard
4 to 5 tablespoons cold water

Mix flour and salt. Cut in shortening. Sprinkle in water, 1 tablespoon at a time, mixing until all flour is moistened and pastry almost cleans side of bowl (1 to 2 teaspoons water can be added).

Gather pastry into ball; shape into flattened round on lightly floured cloth-covered board. (For Two-Crust Pie, divide pastry in half and shape into 2 flattened rounds.) Roll 2 inches larger than inverted pie plate with floured stockinet-covered rolling pin. Fold pastry into quarters; unfold and ease into pie plate.

For One-Crust Pie: Trim overhanging edge of pastry 1 inch from rim of pie plate. Fold and roll pastry even with pie plate; flute.

For Baked Pie Shell: Heat oven to 475°. Prick bottom and side of pastry thoroughly with fork. Bake 8 to 10 minutes.

For Two-Crust Pie: Turn filling into pastry-lined pie plate. Trim overhanging edge of pastry ½ inch from rim of pie plate. Roll other round of pastry. Fold into quarters; cut slits so steam can escape. Place over filling and unfold. Trim overhanging edge of pastry 1 inch from rim of pie plate. Fold and roll top edge under lower edge, pressing on rim to seal; flute.

*If using self-rising flour, omit salt. Pie crusts made with self-rising flour differ in flavor and texture from those made with plain flour.

FRESH BLUEBERRY TART

1 cup all-purpose flour
2 tablespoons granulated sugar
⅛ teaspoon salt
½ cup butter or margarine,
    softened
1 tablespoon white vinegar

1 cup granulated sugar
2 tablespoons flour
¼ teaspoon ground cinnamon
3 cups blueberries
2 tablespoons powdered sugar

Mix 1 cup flour, 2 tablespoons granulated sugar, the salt and butter with hands. Stir in vinegar. Press dough evenly on bottom and 1 inch up side of ungreased 9-inch loose-bottom layer pan or 9-inch springform pan. Be sure no thin areas appear at bottom seam of pan. Refrigerate at least 15 minutes.

Heat oven to 400°. Mix 1 cup granulated sugar, 2 tablespoons flour and the cinnamon. Stir in 2 cups of the blueberries gently, reserving 1 cup of the largest berries. Spread filling evenly over crust.

Bake until crust is golden brown, 50 to 60 minutes. Sprinkle with reserved berries and powdered sugar. Cool and remove pan rim. 6 TO 8 SERVINGS.

NOTE: Tart can be baked in baking pan, 8x8x2 inches.

CARROT PIE

4 cups sliced uncooked carrots
    (about 1 pound)
Pastry for 9-inch One-Crust Pie
    (page 42)
2 eggs
¾ cup packed light brown
    sugar

½ teaspoon salt
½ teaspoon ground cinnamon
½ teaspoon ground nutmeg
¼ teaspoon ground cloves
¼ teaspoon ground allspice
1 cup evaporated milk
2 tablespoons honey

Heat 1 inch water to boiling in 2-quart saucepan. Add carrots. Cover and heat to boiling; reduce heat. Cook until carrot slices are very tender, 15 to 20 minutes; drain. Press carrot slices through sieve to measure 2 cups pulp. (Or place in blender container. Cover and blend until uniform consistency.) Cool.

Heat oven to 400°. Prepare pastry. Beat eggs slightly; beat in carrot pulp and remaining ingredients. Pour into pastry-lined pie plate. Cover edge with 3-inch strip of aluminum foil to prevent excessive browning.

Bake 30 minutes; remove foil. Bake until filling is set, 10 to 15 minutes. Cool slightly. Serve warm or refrigerate. Nice served with sweetened whipped cream.

APPLE PANDOWDY

6 medium tart apples, pared
    and thinly sliced (about 6
    cups)
½ cup sugar
½ teaspoon ground cinnamon
¼ teaspoon salt
¼ teaspoon ground nutmeg
½ cup maple-flavored syrup or
    light molasses
3 tablespoons water

2 tablespoons butter or
    margarine, melted
1¼ cups all-purpose flour
¼ teaspoon salt
⅓ cup shortening
3 tablespoons milk
3 tablespoons butter or
    margarine, melted
Cream

Heat oven to 350°. Mix apples, sugar, cinnamon, ¼ teaspoon salt and the nutmeg. Turn into ungreased 2-quart casserole. Mix syrup, water and 2 tablespoons butter; pour over apple mixture.

Mix flour and ¼ teaspoon salt. Cut in shortening. Sprinkle in milk, 1 tablespoon at a time, mixing until all flour is moistened and pastry almost cleans side of bowl.

Gather pastry into ball; shape into flattened round on lightly floured cloth-covered board. Roll round to fit top of casserole with floured stockinet-covered rolling pin. Place over apples in casserole; brush with 3 tablespoons melted butter.

Bake 30 minutes; remove from oven. Cut crust into small pieces with sharp knife, mixing pieces into apple filling. Bake until apples are tender and pieces of crust are golden, about 30 minutes. Serve hot with cream.   6 SERVINGS.

APPLE DEEP DISH PIE

Pastry for 9-inch One-Crust Pie
    (page 42)
1½ cups sugar
½ cup all-purpose flour*
1 teaspoon ground nutmeg
1 teaspoon ground cinnamon

¼ teaspoon salt
12 cups thinly sliced pared
    apples (about 12 medium)
2 tablespoons butter or
    margarine

Heat oven to 425°. Prepare pastry as directed except—roll into 10-inch square. Fold in half; cut slits near center. Mix sugar, flour, nutmeg, cinnamon and salt; toss with apples. Turn into ungreased square pan, 9x9x2 inches. Dot with butter. Cover with crust that has slits cut in it; fold edges under just inside edges of pan. Bake until juice begins to bubble through slits in crust, about 1 hour. Serve warm.   9 SERVINGS.

*If using self-rising flour, omit salt.

Pictured opposite.
Apples in abundance—and in a variety of delicious guises. From left: Apple Pandowdy (this page), Candy Apples on Sticks (page 152), Apple Butter (page 120) and Apple Dumplings (page 46).

APPLE DUMPLINGS

2 cups all-purpose flour*
2 teaspoons baking powder
1 teaspoon salt
¾ cup shortening
½ cup milk
6 baking apples (each about 3
  inches in diameter), pared
  and cut into quarters

6 tablespoons sugar
Ground cinnamon
Ground nutmeg
Syrup (below)
Whipping cream

Heat oven to 375°. Mix flour, baking powder and salt. Cut in short-ening. Stir in milk until all flour is moistened. Gather pastry into ball. Roll ⅔ of the pastry into 14-inch square on generously floured cloth-covered board with floured stockinet-covered rolling pin; cut into 4 squares. Roll remaining pastry into rectangle, 14x7 inches; cut into 2 squares.

Place 4 apple quarters on each pastry square. Sprinkle each with 1 tablespoon sugar, the cinnamon and nutmeg. Bring corners of pastry up over apple and press together. Place dumplings in ungreased baking pan, 13x9x2 inches. Pour Syrup over dumplings.

Bake until crust is golden and apples are tender, about 45 minutes. Spoon Syrup over dumplings. Serve warm with cream.   6 SERVINGS.

*If using self-rising flour, omit baking powder and salt.

SYRUP

2 cups sugar
¼ teaspoon ground cinnamon
¼ teaspoon ground nutmeg

2 cups water
¼ cup butter or margarine

Heat sugar, cinnamon, nutmeg and water to boiling. Remove from heat; stir in butter until melted.

MINCEMEAT-PUMPKIN PIE

Pastry for 9-inch One-Crust Pie
  (page 42)
½ cup sugar
½ teaspoon ground cinnamon
¼ teaspoon salt

¼ teaspoon ground nutmeg
1½ cups prepared mincemeat
1 cup canned pumpkin
½ cup milk
2 eggs, beaten

Heat oven to 425°. Prepare pastry. Mix sugar, cinnamon, salt, nut-meg, mincemeat and pumpkin. Stir in milk and eggs. Pour into pastry-lined pie plate. Cover edge with 3-inch strip of aluminum foil to prevent excessive browning.

Bake 25 minutes; remove foil. Bake until top is golden brown, 10 to 15 minutes. Cool slightly. Serve warm or refrigerate.

To someone from the South, nothing compares with a luscious peach pie—except perhaps Pecan Pie when the short season for local peaches is over. Both of these pies can be served in the traditional way—with a liberal dollop of whipped cream. But try them also in that all-American fashion, a la mode, with a scoop of your favorite ice cream on top.

PEACH CRUMBLE PIE

Pastry for 9-inch One-Crust Pie
  (page 42)
4 cups quartered peeled
  peaches (8 to 10 medium)
½ cup granulated sugar
½ teaspoon ground nutmeg
2 tablespoons cream

1 egg
½ cup all-purpose flour
¼ cup packed brown sugar
¼ teaspoon ground cinnamon
¼ teaspoon ground nutmeg
¼ cup butter or margarine,
  softened

Heat oven to 425°. Prepare pastry. Arrange peaches in pastry-lined pie plate. Mix granulated sugar and ½ teaspoon nutmeg; sprinkle over peaches. Beat cream and egg; pour over peaches. Mix flour, brown sugar, cinnamon, ¼ teaspoon nutmeg and the butter until crumbly; sprinkle over peaches. Cover edge with 3-inch strip of aluminum foil to prevent excessive browning.

Bake 30 minutes; remove foil. Bake until top is golden brown, 5 to 10 minutes. Cool slightly. Serve warm.

PECAN PIE

Pastry for 9-inch One-Crust Pie
  (page 42)
½ cup packed dark brown
  sugar*
1 tablespoon flour
¼ teaspoon salt
1 cup light corn syrup

1 tablespoon butter or
  margarine, melted
2 eggs
1 teaspoon vanilla
1½ cups pecan halves (5½
  ounces)

Heat oven to 350°. Prepare pastry. Beat sugar, flour, salt, corn syrup, butter, eggs and vanilla with hand beater. Stir in pecans. Pour into pastry-lined pie plate.

Bake until filling is set, 45 to 55 minutes. Cool slightly. Serve warm or refrigerate.

*½ cup granulated sugar and 1 cup dark corn syrup can be substituted for the dark brown sugar and light corn syrup.

Chocolate Pecan Pie: Melt 2 squares (1 ounce each) unsweetened chocolate with the butter.

Arizona, Florida and California grow most of our year-round citrus crops. A large portion of the lime crop grows in Florida, and one variety favored for pies only grows down in the humid Florida Keys. Their famous Key Lime Pie that swept the country in the late nineteenth century was invented soon after condensed milk, one of its main ingredients, began to be canned in 1858. Since then lime pies of all types—and lemon, too—have become American classics.

DOUBLE-CRUST LEMON PIE

2 large lemons
2 cups sugar
1 teaspoon salt

Pastry for 9-inch Two-Crust
Pie (page 42)
4 eggs

Grate 2 teaspoons peel from lemons. Peel lemons, removing all white membrane. Cut lemons into very thin slices; place in bowl. Stir in lemon peel, sugar and salt.

Heat oven to 425°. Prepare pastry. Beat eggs thoroughly; pour over lemon slice mixture and mix well. Pour into pastry-lined pie plate. Cover with top crust that has slits cut in it; seal and flute. Cover edge with 3-inch strip of aluminum foil to prevent excessive browning.

Bake 35 minutes; remove foil. Bake until knife inserted near edge of pie comes out clean, 10 to 15 minutes. Cool slightly and refrigerate.

LIME CHIFFON PIE

9-inch Baked Pie Shell (page 42)
½ cup sugar
1 envelope unflavored gelatin
4 eggs, separated
⅔ cup water
⅓ cup lime juice (about 2
    limes)

1 tablespoon grated lime peel
Few drops green food color
    (optional)
½ teaspoon cream of tartar
½ cup sugar

Bake pie shell; cool. Mix ½ cup sugar and the gelatin in 1-quart saucepan. Mix egg yolks, water and lime juice; stir into sugar mixture. Cook over medium heat, stirring constantly, just until mixture boils. Stir in lime peel and food color. Chill in bowl of ice and water or in refrigerator, stirring occasionally, until mixture mounds slightly when dropped from spoon.

Beat egg whites and cream of tartar until foamy. Beat in ½ cup sugar, 1 tablespoon at a time; continue beating until stiff and glossy. Do not underbeat. Fold lime mixture into meringue; pile into pie shell. Refrigerate until set, at least 3 hours.

RHUBARB AND STRAWBERRY PIE

Pastry for 9-inch Two-Crust
  Pie (page 42)
1½ cups sugar
2 tablespoons quick-cooking
  tapioca

¼ teaspoon salt
2 cups ½-inch pieces rhubarb
2 cups strawberries
1 egg yolk, slightly beaten

Heat oven to 425°. Prepare pastry. Mix sugar, tapioca and salt; toss with rhubarb and strawberries. Stir in egg yolk. Turn into pastry-lined pie plate. Cover with top crust that has slits cut in it; seal and flute. Cover edge with 3-inch strip of aluminum foil to prevent excessive browning.

Bake 30 minutes; remove foil. Bake until crust is golden brown and juice begins to bubble through slits in crust, 10 to 15 minutes.

The distant ancestors of Fried Pies were oilcakes—fried, fruit-stuffed sweet rolls often served at Mount Vernon. Since fritters and fried pies cook quickly, cooks long ago discovered how handy they are for last-minute desserts.

FRIED PIES

1 package (12 ounces) mixed
  dried fruit
2 to 3 tablespoons sugar
¾ teaspoon ground cinnamon
½ teaspoon ground nutmeg
2 cups all-purpose flour*

1 teaspoon baking powder
½ teaspoon salt
¼ cup shortening
½ cup milk
1 egg, slightly beaten

Remove prune pits; cut up fruit. Heat fruit and enough water to cover to boiling; reduce heat. Cover and simmer until pears are tender, 20 to 25 minutes; drain. Stir in sugar, cinnamon and nutmeg.

Mix flour, baking powder and salt. Cut in shortening. Mix milk and egg; stir into flour mixture until all flour is moistened and pastry almost cleans side of bowl. Gather pastry into ball; divide in half. Roll each half ⅛ to ¹/₁₆ inch thick on lightly floured cloth-covered board with floured stockinet-covered rolling pin. Cut each half into four 6-inch rounds. Place ¼ cup fruit mixture on each round. Moisten lower edge of round; fold pastry over. Press edges firmly with fork to seal securely.

Heat vegetable oil or shortening (3 to 4 inches) to 375° in deep fat fryer or heavy saucepan. Fry pies in hot oil until golden brown on both sides, 3 to 4 minutes; drain on paper towels.   8 PIES.

*If using self-rising flour, omit baking powder and salt.

CHESS PIE

Pastry for 8-inch One-Crust Pie
   (page 42)
1 cup sugar
1 tablespoon flour
¼ cup butter or margarine,
   softened

5 egg yolks
½ cup light cream (20%)
⅛ teaspoon salt

Heat oven to 400°. Prepare pastry. Beat sugar, flour, butter and egg yolks until smooth. Stir in cream and salt. Pour into pastry-lined pie plate.

Bake 10 minutes. Reduce oven temperature to 325°. Bake until top is golden and center is set, about 30 minutes. Cool slightly. Serve warm or refrigerate.

SOUTHERN PEANUT BUTTER PIE

Pastry for 9-inch One-Crust Pie
   (page 42)
⅔ cup sugar
½ teaspoon salt

1 cup dark corn syrup
⅓ cup creamy peanut butter
3 eggs
1 cup salted peanuts

Heat oven to 375°. Prepare pastry. Beat sugar, salt, corn syrup, peanut butter and eggs; stir in peanuts. Pour into pastry-lined pie plate.

Bake until pastry is golden brown, 40 to 50 minutes. (Center of filling may be slightly soft but will become firm as pie cools.) Cool slightly and refrigerate. Nice served with sweetened whipped cream or ice cream.

VINEGAR PIE

8-inch Baked Pie Shell (page 42)
1 cup sugar
2 tablespoons flour
2 tablespoons cider vinegar
2 eggs, beaten

1 tablespoon butter or
   margarine
½ teaspoon lemon extract
Sweetened whipped cream

Bake pie shell; cool. Mix sugar and flour in 2-quart saucepan. Add enough water to vinegar to measure 1 cup; blend into eggs. Stir egg mixture gradually into sugar mixture. Cook over medium heat, stirring constantly, until mixture thickens and boils. Boil and stir 1 minute. Remove from heat; stir in butter and lemon extract. Cool slightly. Pour into pie shell; refrigerate. Serve with whipped cream.

Pictured opposite.
Each of these pies reflects the character and charm of the South. From top: Southern Peanut Butter Pie (this page), Lime Chiffon Pie (page 48) and Chess Pie (this page).

BLACK BOTTOM PIE

9-inch Baked Pie Shell (page 42)
½ cup sugar
2 tablespoons cornstarch
½ teaspoon salt
2 cups milk
2 eggs, separated
2 teaspoons unflavored gelatin

3 tablespoons cold water
2 tablespoons rum or 2
  teaspoons rum flavoring
1 ounce melted unsweetened
  chocolate (cool)
¼ teaspoon cream of tartar
⅓ cup sugar

Bake pie shell; cool. Mix ½ cup sugar, the cornstarch and salt in 2-quart saucepan. Mix milk and egg yolks; stir gradually into sugar mixture. Cook over medium heat, stirring constantly, until mixture thickens and boils. Boil and stir 1 minute. Reserve 1 cup of the custard mixture. Sprinkle gelatin on cold water to soften; stir into remaining hot mixture in saucepan. Stir in rum. Chill in bowl of ice and water or in refrigerator, stirring occasionally, until mixture mounds slightly when dropped from spoon. Mix chocolate and the reserved custard mixture; pour into baked pie shell.

Beat egg whites and cream of tartar until foamy. Beat in ⅓ cup sugar, 1 tablespoon at a time; continue beating until stiff and glossy. Do not underbeat. Fold gelatin mixture into meringue. Spread over chocolate mixture. Refrigerate until set, at least 3 hours. Spread sweetened whipped cream over pie and sprinkle with shaved chocolate if desired.

SHOOFLY PIE

Pastry for 9-inch One-Crust Pie
  (page 42)
¾ cup all-purpose flour*
½ cup packed brown sugar
½ teaspoon salt
½ teaspoon ground cinnamon
¼ teaspoon ground ginger

⅛ teaspoon ground nutmeg
3 tablespoons butter or
  margarine
¾ cup hot water
½ teaspoon baking soda
½ cup dark molasses
1 egg yolk, well beaten

Pictured opposite.
Five mainstays of American cooking, each with a heritage all its own. From top: Stuffed Green Peppers (page 66), Country Captain (page 75), Barbecued Spareribs (page 67), Manhattan Clam Chowder (page 57) and Yankee Pot Roast of Beef (page 65).

Heat oven to 400°. Prepare pastry. Mix flour, sugar, salt, cinnamon, ginger, nutmeg and butter with hands until crumbly. Mix water and baking soda in 1-quart bowl. Stir in molasses and egg yolk. Pour into pastry-lined pie plate. Sprinkle crumbly mixture over molasses mixture. Bake 15 minutes. Reduce oven temperature to 325°. Bake until crust and crumbs are brown, about 20 minutes. Serve warm.

*If using self-rising flour, omit salt.

MAINSTAYS

MAINSTAYS

In Mainstays, American cooking is at its most originally American. What could be more native than Red Flannel Hash, Barbecued Spareribs or Maryland Crab Cakes? It is in Mainstays, too, that regional cookery is most evident. The Codfish Cakes and Clam Chowder of New England, Chili Con Carne from the Southwest, Jambalaya and Brunswick Stew from the South, the West's Beef Pot Roast, Western Style, and Cioppino—each region's main courses transplant easily to dinner tables all over the country. The center of attraction is not, of course, always meat or fish. Slow-baking bean dishes and soups, with their indescribable aura of comfort, have long been nourishing American Mainstays, too.

Early Americans enjoyed an abundance of game, freshwater fish and seafood. Maine lobster, which is such a treat for us today, was once ordinary enough that residents along the coast were almost embarrassed to serve it to guests. Certain West Coast clams, which now are rare, used to be so common that they were loaded onto carts to be fed to chickens and pigs. Bear, squirrel, buffalo, seal, opossum, venison and dozens of game birds are some of the robust meats that were considered standard fare in different parts of the country. In Europe, throughout history, meat was scarce for all but the wealthy. When colonists came to America they encountered a greater variety and quantity of meat than they'd ever dreamed possible. Even more than either fruits and vegetables, it is the availability of meat that contributes to the garden of paradise tone in the early descriptions of American food.

The most famous beef in this country grew from the few head of cattle Spanish explorers brought over for their missions. From the cows that wandered away from the mission lands, the huge roving herds of the West developed. Later replaced by meatier breeds, the longhorn is an almost legendary creature said to once have had a horn span up to seven feet and the ability to smell water miles away. Nothing in the history of our westward expansion, not even the gold rush, compares with the lore of the cowboys and the raw cowtowns where cattle were loaded onto trains and taken to city stockyards.

Before the railroads began transporting beef all over the country, the most plentiful meat was pork. Pigs were easy for farm families to raise and almost every part was useful. After the hams and chops came spareribs, bacon, sausage, headcheese, scrapple and cracklings. Chicken, at that time, was grown commercially only on a small scale. Families valued their hens and served chicken as a special Sunday dinner or for guests. Poultry, cows and sheep were valuable for eggs, milk or wool, but pigs were raised exclusively for food.

Fish were even more plentiful than meat. In the early years along the Atlantic coast, survival often depended on fishing and on digging clams. The Massachusetts and Chesapeake Bays teemed with fish when settlers first arrived on their shores. Cod, particularly, was the staple of New Englanders. It has been known, then and now, as "The Sacred Cod" for several reasons. Traditionally it was believed by the Pilgrims to be the miracle fish that Christ used when he fed the

The cowboy is still a necessary link in today's streamlined beef-processing chain.

multitudes. The indentations on the fish's body were said to be Christ's thumb and finger marks. More practically, the cod was sacred because it was the source of life and livelihood for so many settlers.

Another plentiful saltwater fish was the native American shad. Writers of the time claimed that such large schools traveled up the Hudson River it was hard to catch anything other than shad. Like lobster, the shad wasn't appreciated until its numbers began to decline. By the end of the Revolutionary War, fishermen noticed that the quantity of seafood was declining. Some thought the booms of cannon fire drove the fish away, but it is more likely that the effects of overfishing had begun.

Until refrigeration became common, whatever fish or meats were available had to be prepared immediately or smoked, pickled or salted for storage. Fish usually were salted or dried, as they had been for hundreds of years, but meats were treated in many ways. The hickory-smoked taste we still esteem was developed as a way to delay spoilage. The pungent flavor of corned beef is from the preservation method of pickling with spices. From the Indians, settlers learned to make jerky, dried beef or buffalo strips.

Thanks to refrigeration, meat and fish cookery are simple today. We can buy the exact quantity we need any time of year. The challenge now, in preparation of main courses, is cost. Meat is the highest priced item on the food budget. Fish, especially shellfish, are becoming scarce, and therefore more costly. With this in mind, our selection of Mainstays emphasizes ways of stretching the budget. Soups, stews and dried bean dishes are traditional ways of doing this, with recipes such as Boston Baked Beans or Pennsylvania Dutch Chicken and Corn Soup. Thrifty American cooks also can rely on Family Meat Loaf, Yankee Pot Roast of Beef, Tuna-Cheese Burgers and Hot Chicken Salad. Not that we've forgotten the glories of the American table—the Broiled Marinated Leg of Lamb, Publick House Lobster Pie, Stuffed Pork Chops and many others.

We have chosen not to include those great national favorites, the hot dog and the hamburger, in their classic forms. So completely are they a part of everyday menus that we felt anyone old enough to turn on the stove must know several ways of preparing them! But we have included Corn Dogs and Sloppy Joes, both perfect for children's parties because they're different ways of serving what is sure to be popular.

Our Mainstays are divided by the method of cooking: slow-cooking Soups and Stews that used to simmer on the back burners of the old wood-fired stoves; Oven Features, which are easy for the cook and often help you save energy by cooking more than one dish at a time; and Skillet Specialties and Deep Fries, both usually speedy preparations.

Whether delicate or hearty, simple or festive, all these great Mainstays that have been handed down to us still will hold the center of attention on any table.

SOUPS

If dried beans have ever been underestimated in American cooking, now is certainly the time for their rediscovery. Famed in the dining hall of the U.S. Senate, Senate Bean Soup is a sustaining and economical patriotic favorite, just the thing for a tailgate picnic on a brisk autumn day. Bean soup can be elegant, too. Black Bean Soup with its colorful garnishes dispels any lingering aura of the ordinary.

SENATE BEAN SOUP

1 pound dried navy beans
  (about 2 cups)
12 cups water
1 ham bone
1 cup chopped onion
1 cup chopped celery

1 clove garlic, finely chopped
2½ cups mashed cooked
  potatoes
2 teaspoons salt
¼ teaspoon pepper

Heat beans and water to boiling in 5-quart Dutch oven; boil 2 minutes. Remove from heat; cover and let stand 1 hour.

Add ham bone. Heat to boiling; reduce heat. Cover and simmer until beans are tender, about 2 hours. Stir in remaining ingredients. Cover and simmer 1 hour. Remove ham bone; trim ham from bone and stir into soup.   12 TO 14 SERVINGS.

BLACK BEAN SOUP

1 package (7.5 ounces) dried
  black beans
6 cups water
1 ham bone*
2 carrots, sliced
1 cup chopped celery
1 cup chopped onion
2 cloves garlic, finely chopped

1 small dried hot pepper,
  crumbled
1 bay leaf
1 teaspoon salt
6 lemon slices
1 hard-cooked egg, shredded
¼ cup chopped red onion
Dry white wine (optional)

Heat beans and water to boiling in 4-quart Dutch oven; boil 2 minutes. Remove from heat; cover and let stand 1 hour.

Add ham bone. Heat to boiling; reduce heat. Cover and simmer until beans are tender, about 2 hours. Stir in carrots, celery, 1 cup chopped onion, the garlic, pepper, bay leaf and salt. Cover and simmer 1 hour. Remove ham bone and bay leaf. Soup can be pressed through food mill. (Or place in blender container. Cover and blend until uniform consistency.) Trim ham from bone and stir into soup. Serve with lemon slices, shredded egg, ¼ cup chopped red onion and the wine.   6 SERVINGS.

*1 pound smoked pork hocks or ham shank can be substituted for the ham bone.

CHEESE-POTATO SOUP

3 medium potatoes, pared and chopped (about 2 cups)
1 large onion, chopped (about 1 cup)
2 teaspoons instant chicken bouillon

1½ cups water
8 ounces pasteurized process cheese spread loaf, cut up

Heat potatoes, onion, bouillon and water to boiling in 2-quart saucepan. Cover and cook until potatoes are tender, about 10 minutes. Place in blender container; add cheese. Cover and blend until uniform consistency.   4 SERVINGS.

CRAB BISQUE

1 can (11½ ounces) condensed green pea soup
1 can (10¾ ounces) condensed tomato soup
2 cups milk

1 can (6½ ounces) crabmeat, drained and cartilage removed
2 tablespoons dry white wine
Thin lemon slices

Mix soups in 2-quart saucepan. Stir in milk gradually. Stir in crabmeat and wine; heat over low heat, stirring occasionally, but do not boil. Serve with lemon slices.   5 SERVINGS.

MANHATTAN CLAM CHOWDER

¼ cup finely chopped onion
¼ cup finely cut-up lean salt pork
2 cans (6½ ounces each) minced or whole clams,* drained (reserve liquid)
2 cups finely chopped pared uncooked potatoes

⅓ cup chopped celery
1 cup water
1 can (16 ounces) tomatoes
2 teaspoons snipped parsley
1 teaspoon salt
¼ teaspoon dried thyme leaves
⅛ teaspoon pepper

Cook and stir onion and pork until onion is tender and pork is crisp. Stir clam liquid, potatoes, celery and water into onion mixture. Heat to boiling. Cover and cook until potatoes are tender, about 10 minutes. Stir in clams, tomatoes (with liquid), parsley, salt, thyme leaves and pepper. Heat to boiling, stirring occasionally.   4 TO 6 SERVINGS.

*1 pint shucked fresh clams can be substituted for the canned clams. Drain clams, reserving liquid. Chop clams and add with potatoes.

LANDLUBBER'S NEW ENGLAND CLAM CHOWDER

½ cup chopped onion
¼ cup cut-up bacon or lean salt
   pork
2 cans (8 ounces each) minced
   clams, drained (reserve
   liquid)

1 cup finely chopped pared
   uncooked potato
½ teaspoon salt
Dash of pepper
2 cups milk

Cook and stir onion and bacon in 2-quart saucepan until onion is tender and bacon is crisp. Add enough water, if necessary, to reserved clam liquid to measure 1 cup. Stir clams, liquid, potato, salt and pepper into onion mixture. Heat to boiling. Cover and cook until potato is tender, about 15 minutes. Stir in milk; heat until hot, stirring occasionally.   6 SERVINGS.

The essence of one kind of colonial cooking remains intact in the Pennsylvania Dutch countryside of southeastern Pennsylvania. There, the home of Shoofly Pie, scrapple, Apple Butter and pretzels, market day is as colorful as the brightly painted hex signs on the old barns. Shelves of homemade bread and preserves are baked and put up the same way they have been by generations of Pennsylvania Dutch. Their proud, traditional ways of cooking and living endure with virtually no change.

At the end of market day, when the tourists speed back to the cities, the buggies turn toward home and, perhaps, a dinner of scrapple or Chicken and Corn Soup. Our soup has the shortcut of canned corn, but it preserves the Pennsylvania Dutch spirit of combining simple ingredients in a surprising and delicious way.

PENNSYLVANIA DUTCH CHICKEN AND CORN SOUP

4- to 4½-pound stewing
   chicken, cut up
12 cups water
1 medium onion, cut into
   fourths
2 teaspoons salt
1 teaspoon whole mixed
   pickling spice

2 cans (17 ounces each) whole
   kernel corn
1½ cups finely chopped celery
   (with leaves)
2 hard-cooked eggs, chopped
2 teaspoons salt
⅛ teaspoon pepper
Rivels (page 59)

Remove any excess fat from chicken. Heat chicken, giblets, neck, water, onion, 2 teaspoons salt and the pickling spice to boiling; reduce heat. Cover and simmer until thickest pieces of chicken are tender, 2½ to 3 hours. Strain broth. Refrigerate chicken and broth separately.

Remove chicken from bones; remove skin if desired. Cut chicken into small pieces. Remove fat from broth. Heat broth, chicken, corn (with liquid) and celery to boiling; reduce heat. Simmer uncovered 10 minutes. Stir in eggs, 2 teaspoons salt and the pepper. Stir in Rivels. Cover and simmer 7 minutes.   10 TO 12 SERVINGS.

RIVELS
Mix 1 cup all-purpose flour, ¼ teaspoon salt and 1 egg, beaten, until crumbly.

STEWS

Georgia, North Carolina and Virginia all claim to be the birthplace of Brunswick Stew. Since there's no way to settle the dispute, we'll say this is indubitably a Southern specialty and a long-time favorite for church cookouts, political rallies, family reunions and other outdoor gatherings. Squirrel, sometimes a main ingredient, gradually has been replaced with chicken, but Brunswick Stew, like Jambalaya, may vary from place to place and season to season. Long simmering gives Brunswick Stew its memorable flavor.

BRUNSWICK STEW

3- to 3½-pound stewing
   chicken, cut up
4 cups water
1½ teaspoons salt
2 cans (16 ounces each)
   tomatoes
1 can (17 ounces) whole
   kernel corn
1 can (14 ounces) lima beans
1 medium potato, pared and
   cubed (about 1 cup)

1 medium onion, chopped
¼ pound lean salt pork, cut
   into 1-inch pieces
1 teaspoon salt
¼ teaspoon pepper
Dash of cayenne red pepper
½ cup water
2 tablespoons flour

Remove any excess fat from chicken. Heat chicken, giblets, neck, 4 cups water and 1½ teaspoons salt to boiling in 5-quart Dutch oven; reduce heat. Cover and simmer until thickest pieces of chicken are tender, about 1 hour.

Skim fat from broth. Remove chicken from bones if desired. Stir in tomatoes (with liquid), corn (with liquid), beans (with liquid), potato, onion, pork, 1 teaspoon salt, the pepper and red pepper. Heat to boiling; reduce heat. Simmer uncovered 1 hour. Shake ½ cup water and the flour in covered jar. Stir into stew. Heat to boiling, stirring constantly. Boil and stir 1 minute.   8 TO 10 SERVINGS.

When the local ingredients include turtles, crayfish, okra, redfish, sassafras, pecans, lake shrimp, red pepper, chicory and yams and the local residents are Spanish, French, African and a sprinkling of Italian, German and English, an unusual cuisine is bound to evolve.

Creole and Acadian cookery, two strains of native Louisiana cooking, are similar. The city Creoles were families descended from the early Spanish and French; Acadians, commonly called Cajuns, were those French exiles from Acadia (now Nova Scotia) who made their homes in the bayou country.

Even the word *jambalaya* evokes the rhythmic language that the Cajuns still speak, while just a glance at the recipe for Chicken Gumbo reveals something of the lineage of this cuisine. *Gumbo* is an African word for the okra that was brought to America by slaves. Filé powder, added just before serving, is made from dried sassafras leaves. It was originally used as a seasoning by the Choctaws and is used as a thickener and seasoning in many Creole recipes.

CHICKEN GUMBO

3- to 4-pound broiler-fryer chicken, cut up	⅔ cup chopped onion
1 cup chopped celery tops	½ cup chopped green pepper
1 medium onion, sliced	1 can (28 ounces) tomatoes
1 clove garlic, crushed (optional)	¼ cup snipped parsley
1 large bay leaf, crumbled	½ teaspoon red pepper sauce
2 teaspoons salt	1½ cups fresh or frozen okra
2 cups water or chicken broth	⅓ cup uncooked long-grain rice
2 tablespoons butter or margarine	Dash of pepper
	1½ teaspoons filé powder

Remove any excess fat from chicken. Heat chicken, giblets, neck, celery tops, sliced onion, garlic, bay leaf, salt and water to boiling; reduce heat. Cover and simmer until thickest pieces of chicken are done, about 45 minutes. Strain broth. Refrigerate chicken and broth separately.

Remove chicken from bones; remove skin if desired. Cut chicken into pieces. Remove fat from broth. Place broth and chicken pieces in saucepan.

Cook and stir butter, chopped onion and green pepper until onion is tender but not brown. Stir green pepper mixture, tomatoes (with liquid), parsley and pepper sauce into chicken and broth. Heat to boiling; reduce heat. Simmer uncovered 15 minutes. Stir in okra, rice and pepper; simmer 20 minutes. Remove from heat; stir in filé powder. (Soup can be prepared ahead; stir in filé powder after reheating.)   4 TO 6 SERVINGS.

Pictured opposite.
Two hearty main dishes from the Louisiana bayou country. From top: Chicken Gumbo (this page) and Jambalaya (page 84).

OLD-FASHIONED BEEF STEW

¼ cup all-purpose flour
1½ teaspoons salt
⅛ teaspoon pepper
1½ pounds beef stew meat, cut into 1½-inch pieces
2 tablespoons shortening
⅓ cup chopped onion
3 cups hot water
1 can (8½ ounces) small white whole onions, drained, or 2 medium onions, cut into fourths

3 medium potatoes, pared and cut into fourths
2 carrots, cut into 1-inch slices
½ cup fresh, frozen or canned green peas
1 beef bouillon cube
Snipped parsley

Mix flour, salt and pepper. Coat beef with flour mixture. Heat shortening in 4-quart Dutch oven until melted; brown beef. Stir in chopped onion. Cook 5 minutes, stirring frequently; drain off fat.

Add hot water. Heat to boiling; reduce heat. Cover and simmer 2 hours. Stir in remaining ingredients except parsley.

Cover and simmer until vegetables are tender, about 30 minutes. Thicken stew if desired: Shake ½ cup cold water and 1 to 2 tablespoons flour in tightly covered jar. Stir into stew. Heat to boiling, stirring constantly. Boil and stir 1 minute. Sprinkle with parsley. 4 TO 6 SERVINGS.

A pot of lima beans with ham is reminiscent of a time when there was always a pot simmering on the back burner. Pork hock, a cut from the foreleg, is flavorful and inexpensive.

LIMA BEANS WITH PORK HOCKS

2 pounds smoked pork hocks
6 cups water
1 pound dried lima beans (about 2 cups)
1 large onion, chopped

1½ teaspoons dry mustard
1 to 3 dried hot peppers
1 clove garlic, finely chopped
Salt
Pepper

Heat pork hocks and water to boiling in 4-quart Dutch oven; reduce heat. Cover and simmer 30 minutes. Add beans. Heat to boiling; boil 2 minutes. Add onion, mustard, hot peppers and garlic. Heat to boiling; reduce heat. Cover and simmer until beans are tender, 1 to 1¼ hours. Add enough water, if necessary, to keep beans covered while simmering. Remove hocks; trim pork from bones and stir into beans. Season with salt and pepper.   6 SERVINGS.

Although most people assume chili is a Mexican import, the fact is that it is a product of the Southwest. It has been avidly discussed and devoured there for over a hundred years. Today, there is even a large organization for chili lovers in Texas, the state where everyone knows what you mean when you order "a bowl of red." No self-respecting Texan would add beans to his *chili con carne* (chili with meat), but if you're not a purist, it certainly is a good way to stretch the protein.

CHILI CON CARNE

2 pounds dried pinto beans
    (about 4 cups)
12 cups water
1 tablespoon plus 2 teaspoons
    salt
2 cloves garlic, finely chopped

1 large bay leaf
2 pounds lean ground beef
2 medium onions, sliced
1 cup tomato juice
3 tablespoons chili powder
1½ teaspoons ground cumin

Heat beans and water to boiling in 6-quart Dutch oven; boil 2 minutes. Remove from heat; cover and let stand 1 hour.

Stir in salt, garlic and bay leaf. Heat to boiling; reduce heat. Cover and simmer until beans are tender, 1 to 1½ hours. Discard bay leaf.

Cook and stir ground beef and onions until beef is brown. Stir beef mixture, tomato juice, chili powder and cumin into beans. Heat to boiling; reduce heat. Cover and simmer 1 hour.   10 SERVINGS.

OYSTER STEW

¼ cup butter or margarine
1 pint oysters, drained*
2 cups milk
½ cup light cream (20%)
½ cup fresh or bottled clam
    liquid

1 teaspoon salt
Dash of cayenne red pepper
Dash of Worcestershire sauce
Paprika
Oyster crackers (optional)

Heat butter in 8-inch skillet until melted. Add oysters. Cook and stir over low heat just until edges curl. Heat milk, cream and clam liquid in 2-quart saucepan. Stir in salt, red pepper, Worcestershire sauce and oysters. Sprinkle with paprika. Serve with crackers.   4 SERVINGS.

*The oyster liquid can be substituted for the clam liquid.

Fisherman's Wharf in San Francisco, where tourists stroll along the water eating sourdough bread and feasting on fresh crab and shrimp from paper cups, is lined with seafood restaurants that serve a more sophisticated fare. Cioppino, for example, is a California invention that varies with the day's catch or the fish-market specials. A feast for the eye as well as the palate, Cioppino exhibits several unique attributes of California cooking. Because of the olive groves and vineyards, olive oil and wine are staples of cooking in most of the Far West. Herbs and spices are used generously, perhaps a heritage from the Mexicans, Spanish, Russians and Chinese.

The Mexican and Spanish cooking of the early Western settlers was enhanced by the Russian seal hunters who were attracted to the coast. After the waves of pioneers began to infiltrate the West, thousands of Chinese laborers were brought in to help finish the transcontinental railroad. Thus, an astonishing melting pot occurred in the West, and experimentation in cooking developed as a norm rather than as an exception. The addition, for instance, of prunes and olives in Beef Pot Roast, Western Style, is the kind of imaginative flair that Westerners typically bring to day-to-day fare.

Trawlers ply the seas in every kind of weather to bring back the fixin's for delicious dishes like Cioppino (this page).

CIOPPINO

3 pounds dressed firm saltwater
    fish (sea bass, halibut,
    haddock, turbot)
1 live Dungeness crab
1 pound large raw shrimp
12 clams, oysters or mussels
    (or combination)
2 large onions, chopped (about
    2 cups)
1 large green pepper, chopped
    (about 1 cup)

¼ cup olive oil
1 can (28 ounces) tomatoes
2 cups tomato juice
1 to 2 teaspoons salt
½ teaspoon dried basil leaves
⅛ teaspoon pepper
2 cloves garlic, finely chopped
1 bay leaf
2 cups dry red wine
Snipped parsley

Cut fish into serving pieces. Crack crab. Peel and devein shrimp. Steam clams to open; remove top shells and reserve liquid. Place fish and crab in 8-quart Dutch oven; reserve shrimp and clams.

Cook and stir onions, green pepper and oil in 3-quart saucepan until onions are tender. Stir in reserved clam liquid, tomatoes (with liquid), tomato juice, salt, basil, pepper, garlic and bay leaf. Heat to boiling; reduce heat. Simmer uncovered 10 minutes. Stir in wine; pour over fish and crab. Heat to boiling; reduce heat. Cover and simmer 20 minutes. Add shrimp. Cover and simmer 5 minutes. Arrange clams on the half shells on top. Cover and simmer 3 minutes. Sprinkle with parsley. 6 TO 10 SERVINGS.

YANKEE POT ROAST OF BEEF

¼ cup all-purpose flour
2 teaspoons salt
½ teaspoon pepper
4- to 5-pound boneless beef
    shoulder pot roast
1 tablespoon shortening
½ cup water
2 cups sliced celery

3 medium potatoes, pared and
    cut into ½-inch cubes
    (about 2 cups)
2 cups diced carrots
2 cups ½-inch cubes rutabaga
    or yellow turnips
1 cup chopped onion

Mix flour, salt and pepper; rub over beef roast. Heat shortening in skillet or Dutch oven until melted; brown beef on all sides. Drain off fat; add water. Heat to boiling; reduce heat. Cover tightly and simmer on top of range or in 325° oven 2 hours.

Add vegetables. Add ¼ cup water if necessary. Cover and simmer until beef and vegetables are tender, 45 to 60 minutes. 12 TO 16 SERVINGS.

Across the country, the variations on pot roast are as distinctive as local accents. Chances are you have your own idea of the way pot roast should be prepared. For a change, however, try it with these Yankee or Western overtones.

BEEF POT ROAST, WESTERN STYLE

1 cup water
1 cup pitted prunes
    (about ½ pound)*
2 teaspoons salt
½ teaspoon ground ginger
¼ teaspoon pepper
4- to 5-pound boneless
    beef shoulder pot roast
1 tablespoon shortening

1½ cups chopped onion
2 cloves garlic, finely
    chopped
½ cup water or dry red
    wine
1 can (6 ounces) pitted
    ripe olives, drained
5 ounces mushrooms, sliced
    (about 2 cups)

Pour 1 cup water over prunes; reserve. Mix salt, ginger and pepper; rub over beef roast. Heat shortening in skillet or Dutch oven until melted; brown beef on all sides. Drain off fat; add onion, garlic and water. Heat to boiling; reduce heat. Cover tightly and simmer on top of range or in 325° oven 2 hours.

Add prunes, olives and mushrooms. Cover and cook until beef is tender, about 1 hour. 12 TO 16 SERVINGS.

*1 cup dried apricots, cut in halves, can be substituted for the prunes.

OVEN FEATURES

FAMILY MEAT LOAF

1 can (16 ounces) tomatoes
2 pounds ground beef
2 eggs
1 cup old-fashioned oats

2 teaspoons salt
¼ teaspoon pepper
¼ teaspoon ground nutmeg

Place tomatoes (with liquid) in blender container. Cover and blend 5 seconds on low speed. Mix all ingredients; spread evenly in ungreased loaf pan, 9x5x3 inches. Bake uncovered in 350° oven until done, about 1½ hours. Drain off fat once during baking.   8 SERVINGS.

STUFFED GREEN PEPPERS

6 large green peppers
1 pound ground beef
2 tablespoons chopped
    onion
1 teaspoon salt

⅛ teaspoon garlic salt
1 cup cooked rice
1 can (15 ounces) tomato
    sauce

Heat oven to 350°. Cut thin slice from stem end of each pepper. Remove all seeds and membranes. Cook peppers in boiling salted water (½ teaspoon salt to 1 cup water) 5 minutes; drain. Cook and stir ground beef and onion in 10-inch skillet until beef is brown and onion is tender; drain off fat. Stir in salt, garlic salt, rice and 1 cup of the tomato sauce; heat until rice is hot. Stuff each pepper lightly with ½ cup beef mixture. Stand peppers upright in baking dish, 8x8x2 inches. Pour on remaining tomato sauce. Cover with foil and bake 45 minutes. Remove foil and bake 15 minutes.   6 SERVINGS.

SPICY CORNED BEEF

4-pound beef corned brisket
1 tablespoon whole mixed
    pickling spice
1 medium onion, cut into
    fourths
1 carrot, cut in half

1 stalk celery, cut in half
⅓ cup packed brown sugar
1 tablespoon prepared brown
    mustard
½ cup sweet pickle juice

Cover beef corned brisket with cold water. Add pickling spice, onion, carrot and celery. Heat to boiling; reduce heat. Cover and simmer until beef is tender, about 4 hours. Cool beef in broth. Place beef fat side up in ungreased baking pan, 13x9x2 inches. Score fat surface lightly. Mix sugar and mustard; spread over fat. Pour pickle juice into pan. Bake uncovered in 300° oven 1 hour, basting occasionally with pan juices.   8 TO 10 SERVINGS.

Like many culinary terms, the word *barbecue* derives from a description of a method of cooking. In Spanish, *barbacoa* means an elevated framework of sticks, one of the oldest cooking methods and the one most suited to the slow cooking of whole game.

By now the enormous barbecues of the Southwest have been adapted to almost every backyard in America. Is it the ancient appeal of sitting around a campfire, or does food really taste better outdoors?

BARBECUED SPARERIBS

4½ pounds pork spareribs,
   cut into serving pieces

Tomato, Mustard or
   Spicy Barbecue Sauce (below)

Place pork spareribs meaty sides up on rack in shallow roasting pan. Do not add water. Do not cover. Roast in 325° oven 1 hour. Brush spareribs with Tomato Barbecue Sauce. Bake, turning and brushing frequently with sauce, until spareribs are tender, about 45 minutes. 5 OR 6 SERVINGS.

TOMATO BARBECUE SAUCE

1 tablespoon dry mustard
1½ teaspoons onion salt
½ teaspoon garlic powder
⅔ cup catsup
⅓ cup water

¼ cup butter or margarine
2 tablespoons Worcestershire
   sauce
¼ teaspoon red pepper
   sauce

Heat all ingredients, stirring frequently, until butter is melted.

MUSTARD BARBECUE SAUCE

⅓ cup prepared brown
   mustard

⅓ cup molasses
⅓ cup cider vinegar

Mix mustard and molasses; stir in vinegar.

SPICY BARBECUE SAUCE

1 teaspoon sugar
1 teaspoon onion salt
½ teaspoon garlic powder
½ teaspoon pepper
Dash of cayenne red pepper

⅓ cup butter or margarine
2 tablespoons water
2 tablespoons vinegar
1 tablespoon Worcestershire
   sauce

Heat all ingredients, stirring frequently, until butter is melted.

Barbecued Chicken: Cut two 2½- to 3-pound broiler-fryer chickens into serving pieces. Place skin sides up on rack in shallow roasting pan; brush with vegetable oil. Roast in 325° oven 45 minutes. Brush chicken with Tomato Barbecue Sauce. Bake, turning and brushing frequently with sauce, until thickest pieces are done, about 30 minutes. 6 TO 8 SERVINGS.

ROAST PORK LOIN WITH SAGEY ONIONS

4-pound boneless pork top loin
   roast (double)
Salt
Pepper
2 pounds yellow onions

1¼ teaspoons ground sage
1 teaspoon salt
¼ teaspoon pepper
Gravy (below)

Place pork roast fat side up on rack in shallow roasting pan. Sprinkle with salt and pepper. Insert meat thermometer so tip is in center of thickest part of pork and does not rest in fat. Do not add water. Do not cover. Roast in 325° oven 1½ hours.

Heat 2 inches water to boiling. Add onions. Cover and heat to boiling. Cook until tender, 15 to 20 minutes; drain. Chop onions coarsely; stir in sage, 1 teaspoon salt and ¼ teaspoon pepper. Remove pork and rack from pan; pour off drippings, reserving ¼ cup. Mound onion mixture in center of pan; place pork on top. Roast until meat thermometer registers 170°, about 1 hour.   8 SERVINGS.

GRAVY

Mix reserved ¼ cup drippings and ¼ cup all-purpose flour. Cook over low heat, stirring constantly, until mixture is smooth and bubbly. Remove from heat; stir in 2 cups water. Heat to boiling, stirring constantly. Boil and stir 1 minute. Season with salt and pepper.

STUFFED PORK CHOPS

1 jar (14 ounces)
   cranberry-orange relish
2 tablespoons packed brown
   sugar
½ teaspoon salt
4 pork loin chops, 1 inch thick
   (with pockets for stuffing)
2 tablespoons flour

2 teaspoons salt
¼ teaspoon pepper
1 tablespoon shortening
1 large rutabaga (about 2
   pounds), pared and cut into
   ½-inch slices
Salt
¼ cup water

Heat oven to 350°. Mix relish, sugar and ½ teaspoon salt. Spoon 2 tablespoons of the relish mixture into each pork chop pocket; secure opening with wooden picks. Mix flour, 2 teaspoons salt and the pepper; rub over chops. Heat shortening in 10-inch skillet until melted; brown chops on both sides.

Place chops in corners of ungreased baking dish, 13½x8¾x1¾ inches. Layer rutabaga slices in center of baking dish; sprinkle each layer with salt. Pour water into skillet. Stir and scrape brown particles from skillet; pour over chops and rutabaga. Cover baking dish with aluminum foil. Bake until rutabaga is tender and chops are done, about 1½ hours. Serve with remaining relish.   4 SERVINGS.

Pictured opposite.
The farmlands of the Midwest inspired this Sunday dinner specialty—Roast Pork Loin with Sagey Onions.

SCALLOPED POTATOES AND HAM

The regional smokehouse, fragrant with hams, is now mainly a part of our past.

6 medium potatoes, pared
 and thinly sliced (about
 4 cups)
3 tablespoons flour
1 teaspoon salt

¼ teaspoon pepper
1½ cups cubed cooked ham
¼ cup finely chopped onion
¼ cup butter or margarine
2½ cups milk

Heat oven to 350°. Layer ¼ of the potato slices in greased 2-quart casserole; sprinkle each of the first 3 layers with 1 tablespoon flour, ¼ teaspoon salt, dash of pepper, ½ cup ham and 1 tablespoon onion. Dot each layer with 1 tablespoon butter. Sprinkle top with remaining salt, pepper and onion. Dot with remaining butter. Heat milk just to scalding; pour over potato mixture. Cover and bake 30 minutes. Uncover and bake until potatoes are tender, 60 to 70 minutes. Let stand 5 to 10 minutes before serving.   4 TO 6 SERVINGS.

As everyone who grew up on cowboy movies knows, sheep were not welcome in Western grazing lands. Miles of film recorded the shoot-outs between the sheep herders and the cowboys. Today, Colorado and other Western states raise both beef and lamb, so despite the Saturday movies, the dispute was settled.

And lucky for us, for lamb has become an American favorite. Most often it is simply roasted—and a roast leg of lamb is frequently the choice for a spring or Easter feast. In fact, lamb is so delicious in its unadorned preparation that relatively few elaborate variations have developed. Americans have cultivated such a taste for lamb that recipes for mutton are almost unknown here.

In the three selections that follow, lamb proves itself to be a very adaptable meat. Whether barbecued in a spicy sauce, marinated in wine and then broiled, or ground and made into tasty patties, lamb accommodates itself equally well.

BARBECUED BREAST OF LAMB

4 pounds breast of lamb,
 cut into serving pieces
2 medium onions, sliced
2 cloves garlic, finely
 chopped
2 teaspoons salt
2 teaspoons chili powder
¾ cup catsup

¾ cup water
¼ cup plus 1 tablespoon
 cider vinegar
1 tablespoon plus 1 teaspoon
 Worcestershire sauce
¼ teaspoon red pepper
 sauce

Brown lamb in 4-quart Dutch oven; drain off fat. Mix remaining ingredients; pour over lamb. Cover and bake in 350° oven 1¼ hours. Uncover and bake 15 minutes; drain off fat.   6 SERVINGS.

BROILED MARINATED LEG OF LAMB

5- to 8-pound leg of lamb,
  boned and butterflied
2 cups dry red wine
¼ cup vegetable oil
2 teaspoons salt

2 teaspoons dried rosemary
  leaves, crushed
2 cloves garlic, crushed
¼ teaspoon pepper

Place lamb in plastic bag or shallow baking dish. Mix remaining ingredients; pour over lamb. Fasten bag securely or cover dish with plastic wrap. Refrigerate at least 48 hours but no longer than 96 hours, turning lamb occasionally.

Drain lamb, reserving marinade. Slash outer edge of any fat on lamb at 1-inch intervals to prevent curling (do not cut into lamb). Set oven control to broil and/or 550°. Place lamb on rack in broiler pan. Place broiler pan so top of lamb is 5 to 6 inches from heat.

Broil until brown, about 25 minutes, brushing occasionally with reserved marinade. Turn lamb; broil until desired doneness, 20 to 30 minutes, brushing occasionally. Cut lamb across grain into thin slices.   ABOUT 8 SERVINGS.

Broiled Butterflied Leg of Lamb: Omit marinade. Rub lamb with 1 clove garlic; brush with vegetable oil. Slash outer edge of any fat at 1-inch intervals (do not cut into lamb). Broil as directed above.

BEST BROILED LAMB PATTIES

1 pound ground lamb
2 tablespoons dry bread crumbs
1 tablespoon snipped parsley
½ teaspoon salt
¼ teaspoon dill weed

1 egg
1 clove garlic, minced
4 slices bacon
Apricot-Mint Sauce (below)

Mix meat, bread crumbs, parsley, salt, dill weed, egg and garlic. Shape mixture into 4 patties, 1 inch thick and about 3 inches in diameter. Wrap slice of bacon around edge of each patty and secure with wooden picks.

Set oven control at broil and/or 550°. Broil patties 3 inches from heat about 15 minutes, turning once.   4 SERVINGS.

APRICOT-MINT SAUCE
Mix 2 jars (4¾ ounces each) strained apricots (baby food), ¼ cup mint-flavored apple jelly and 1 drop green food color.

BAKED CATFISH

1 dressed catfish (3 to 4
   pounds)*
½ teaspoon salt
⅛ teaspoon pepper
2 cups soft bread cubes
2 tablespoons snipped parsley
1 tablespoon pickle relish
1 small onion, finely chopped

1 egg, beaten
½ teaspoon salt
¼ teaspoon pepper
2 tablespoons butter or
   margarine, melted
6 slices lean salt pork
Broth (below)

Heat oven to 350°. Wash catfish in cold water; pat dry with paper towels. Rub cavity with ½ teaspoon salt and ⅛ teaspoon pepper. Mix bread cubes, parsley, relish, onion, egg, ½ teaspoon salt and ¼ teaspoon pepper; spoon lightly into cavity. Close opening with skewers; lace with string. Brush fish with butter. Cut 3 slits in each side; place a slice of salt pork in each slit. Place fish in greased shallow baking dish. Bake uncovered, spooning Broth over fish occasionally, until fish flakes easily with fork, 45 to 60 minutes. 6 SERVINGS.

*Other large fish such as lake trout, bass, haddock, salmon, whitefish, cod or red snapper can be substituted for the catfish.

BROTH
Heat 1½ cups water, 4 lemon slices, 1 onion slice, 1 bay leaf, crumbled, ½ cup chopped celery tops and 4 peppercorns to boiling; reduce heat. Cover and simmer 20 minutes; strain.

SALMON CASSEROLES

1 can (16 ounces) salmon,
   drained and flaked
½ teaspoon salt
Dash of pepper
2 tablespoons milk
1 egg, slightly beaten
⅔ cup chopped celery

2 tablespoons chopped onion
3 tablespoons shortening
½ teaspoon salt
½ teaspoon ground sage
⅓ cup milk
2 cups soft bread crumbs
4 green pepper rings

Heat oven to 350°. Mix salmon, ½ teaspoon salt, dash of pepper, 2 tablespoons milk and the egg. Press lightly on bottoms and about halfway up sides of 4 greased 10-ounce baking dishes.

Cook and stir celery, onion and shortening in 2-quart saucepan until celery is tender. Stir in ½ teaspoon salt, the sage, ⅓ cup milk and the bread crumbs. Spoon into center of each baking dish, pressing lightly to make celery mixture level with salmon mixture. Bake uncovered 25 minutes. Top each with pepper ring; bake 5 minutes. Nice served with a cheese sauce. 4 SERVINGS.

TUNA-CHEESE BURGERS

1 can (6½ ounces) tuna,
   drained
1 cup chopped celery
½ cup cut-up process
   American cheese
¼ cup finely chopped onion
¼ teaspoon salt
⅛ teaspoon pepper
¼ cup mayonnaise or salad
   dressing
6 hamburger buns
Butter or margarine, softened

Heat oven to 350°. Mix all ingredients except buns and butter. Spread buns with butter. Fill with tuna mixture. Place each sandwich on square of aluminum foil; fold edges securely. Place on baking sheet. Bake until tuna mixture is hot, about 20 minutes. 6 SANDWICHES.

TUNA-NOODLE CASSEROLE

8 ounces uncooked egg noodles
2 cans (6½ ounces each) tuna,
   well drained
1½ cups dairy sour cream
¾ cup milk
1 can (3 ounces) sliced
   mushrooms, drained
1½ teaspoons salt
¼ teaspoon pepper
¼ cup dry bread crumbs
¼ cup grated Parmesan cheese
2 tablespoons butter or
   margarine, melted

Heat oven to 350°. Cook noodles as directed on package; drain. Return noodles to saucepan; stir in tuna, sour cream, milk, mushrooms, salt and pepper. Pour into ungreased 2-quart casserole. Mix bread crumbs, cheese and butter; sprinkle evenly over tuna mixture. Bake uncovered until hot and bubbly, 35 to 40 minutes. 6 TO 8 SERVINGS.

SCALLOPED OYSTERS

2 cups crushed soda crackers
   (about 40 squares)
½ teaspoon salt
⅛ teaspoon pepper
Dash of ground mace
¼ cup butter or margarine,
   melted
1 pint oysters, cut in halves
½ cup half-and-half

Heat oven to 400°. Mix crackers, salt, pepper, mace and butter. Pat half of the cracker mixture evenly in buttered baking dish, 8x8x2 inches. Arrange oysters on cracker mixture. Sprinkle remaining cracker mixture over oysters. Pour half-and-half over top. Bake uncovered until hot, about 20 minutes. 4 OR 5 SERVINGS.

Think of Maine and what comes to mind? Some might say blueberries or the charming scenery of the rocky coast, but for most of us, Maine is synonymous with lobster. The cold water off that state is the ideal home for the awkward and unlikely looking creature that has become America's most luxurious seafood.

Are we to believe the many records about the quantities and sizes of the lobsters our ancestors first hauled out of the Maine waters? Apparently lobsters, which are long-lived creatures, had been undisturbed before the European settlement in America. Many had lived a hundred years and had grown to prodigious lengths. But to imagine a six-foot lobster is to find oneself in the realm of tall tales!

Lobsters, as prices tell us, are the victims of over-demand. Occasionally someone pulls in a twenty-five-pounder, but these days lobsters usually aren't in the water long enough to grow so large. It takes about seven years for a lobster to reach the smallest legal size for catching.

If you've ever noticed that one claw on a lobster is larger than the other, there's a reason: lobsters are either left- or right-handed, and the claw they use becomes more developed.

Although live lobsters are seasonal and not always easy to find, here is an interesting recipe that uses canned lobster meat, available all year long.

PUBLICK HOUSE LOBSTER PIE

¼ cup butter or margarine
2 tablespoons flour
½ teaspoon salt
2 cups half-and-half
2 eggs, slightly beaten
2 cans (5 ounces each) lobster, drained and cut up (2 cups)
½ cup dry white wine

½ cup cracker crumbs
¼ cup crushed potato chips
2 tablespoons grated Parmesan cheese
1 teaspoon paprika
¼ cup butter or margarine, melted

Heat oven to 300°. Heat ¼ cup butter in 2-quart saucepan over low heat until melted. Stir in flour and salt. Cook over low heat, stirring constantly, until mixture is smooth and bubbly. Remove from heat; stir in half-and-half gradually. Heat to boiling, stirring constantly. Boil and stir 1 minute.

Stir at least half of the hot mixture into eggs. Blend egg mixture into hot mixture in saucepan. Cook over medium heat, stirring constantly, 3 minutes. Remove from heat; stir in lobster and wine. Pour into ungreased baking dish, 11¾ x 7½ x 1¾ inches. Mix cracker crumbs, potato chips, cheese, paprika and ¼ cup butter; sprinkle over lobster mixture. Bake uncovered until lobster is hot, about 15 minutes.   4 SERVINGS.

HOT CHICKEN SALAD

2 cups cut-up cooked chicken
  or turkey
2 cups thinly sliced celery
¾ cup mayonnaise or salad
  dressing
2 tablespoons finely chopped
  onion

2 tablespoons capers
1 teaspoon curry powder
½ teaspoon salt
½ cup toasted slivered almonds

Heat oven to 350°. Mix chicken, celery, mayonnaise, onion, capers, curry powder and salt. Spoon into ungreased 1-quart casserole or six 1-cup baking dishes. Sprinkle with almonds. Bake uncovered until chicken mixture is hot, about 20 minutes.   6 SERVINGS.

Was this dish brought to the port of Savannah by a mysterious captain of the spice trade, as Georgians claim, or was it the wild invention of a local cook desperately tired of fried chicken? No one knows the true originator of Country Captain, but many cooks know this bold and pungent dish's appeal for an exciting menu.

COUNTRY CAPTAIN

½ cup all-purpose flour
1 teaspoon salt
¼ teaspoon pepper
2½- to 3-pound broiler-
  fryer chicken, cut up
¼ cup vegetable oil
1 large onion, chopped
1 green pepper, chopped
1 clove garlic, finely
  chopped, or ⅛ teaspoon
  garlic powder

1 can (16 ounces) tomatoes
1½ teaspoons curry
  powder
½ teaspoon dried thyme
  leaves
¼ teaspoon salt
¼ cup currants or raisins
⅓ cup toasted slivered
  blanched almonds
3 cups hot cooked rice

Heat oven to 350°. Mix flour, 1 teaspoon salt and the pepper. Coat chicken with flour mixture. Heat oil in 10-inch skillet. Cook chicken in oil over medium heat until light brown, 15 to 20 minutes. Place chicken in ungreased 2½-quart casserole. Drain oil from skillet.

Add onion, green pepper, garlic, tomatoes (with liquid), curry powder, thyme and ¼ teaspoon salt to skillet. Heat to boiling, stirring frequently to loosen brown particles from skillet. Pour over chicken. Cover and bake until thickest pieces are done, about 40 minutes. Skim fat from liquid if necessary; add currants. Bake 5 minutes. Sprinkle with almonds. Serve with rice. Accompany with grated fresh coconut and chutney if desired.   4 SERVINGS.

Chicken is a traditional mainstay at crowd-size cookouts like this one in Mount Morris, Illinois.

The politician who promises a chicken in every pot probably gets the votes, for chicken always has been an unequivocal winner. Although it once was scarce enough to be reserved for Sunday dinner, now, fortunately, it is usually one of the best bargains at the meat counter. From Juneau to Miami, there are innumerable recipes for preparing this talented bird.

Hot Chicken Salad (page 75) with its touch of curry, gives interest to a light dinner out of doors on a summer evening. Chicken in Cream shares those two attributes busy cooks appreciate: it is both elegant and requires no watching. And what could be more American than Crunchy Oven-fried Chicken?

CHICKEN IN CREAM

½ cup all-purpose flour*
1 teaspoon salt
¼ teaspoon pepper
2½ - to 3-pound broiler-
    fryer chicken, cut up

2 cups light cream (20%)
Paprika

Heat oven to 325°. Mix flour, salt and pepper. Coat chicken with flour mixture. Place skin sides down in ungreased baking dish, 13½x8¾x1¾ inches. Pour cream over chicken. Bake uncovered 45 minutes; turn. Bake until thickest pieces are done, 30 to 45 minutes (do not overbake). Place chicken on warm platter. Stir enough hot water or milk into baking dish, if necessary, to give sauce desired consistency; pour over chicken. Sprinkle with paprika. 4 OR 5 SERVINGS.

*If using self-rising flour, decrease salt to ½ teaspoon.

CRUNCHY OVEN-FRIED CHICKEN

1 cup corn flake cereal
    crumbs
1 teaspoon onion salt
⅛ teaspoon pepper

2½ - to 3-pound broiler-
    fryer chicken, cut up
½ cup butter or
    margarine, melted*

Heat oven to 350°. Mix cereal crumbs, onion salt and pepper. Dip chicken in butter; roll in cereal crumb mixture. Place skin sides up in ungreased baking pan, 13x9x2 inches. Pour remaining butter over chicken. Bake uncovered until thickest pieces are done, 1¼ to 1½ hours. 4 SERVINGS.

*½ cup evaporated milk can be substituted for the butter; use greased pan.

Herbed Chicken: Stir 1 teaspoon crushed dried rosemary, marjoram, tarragon or sage leaves into the melted butter.

Pictured opposite.
Chicken is a traditional choice for American picnics. Complement Crunchy Oven-fried Chicken (this page) with Sunshine Cake (page 21), Fresh Mushroom and Spinach Salad (page 108), Dilled Beans (page 126) and Squash Rolls (page 16).

How did America's most famous bird ever get its un-American name? Early sixteenth-century explorers took the birds, domesticated by the Indians, back to Spain from Mexico long before America was settled. As the popularity of the new bird spread over Europe, most people assumed it had come from the exotic East. The French named it "dinde" (d'Inde), meaning "from India." The Germans thought it was a chicken from Calicut, on the coast of Malabar, and called it "KaleKuttisch Hün." It was the English who decided the strange bird must be from Turkey, possibly as a misunderstanding of the Indian name, "furkee."

Our domestic turkeys are easy to roast and have become a symbol of American holidays. After preparing the turkey and stuffing it just before roasting, heat oven to 325°. Place turkey breast side up on rack in open shallow roasting pan. Brush with shortening, oil or butter. Insert meat thermometer so tip is in thickest part of inside thigh muscle or thickest part of breast meat and does not touch bone. Do not add water. Do not cover. Approximate cooking time for an 8- to 12-pound turkey is 3½ to 4½ hours, for a 12- to 16-pound turkey, 4½ to 5½ hours. Meat thermometer should register 185°. When turkey is done, remove from oven and allow to stand about 20 minutes for easiest carving. As soon as possible after serving, remove every bit of stuffing from turkey. Cool stuffing, meat and any gravy promptly; refrigerate and use within two days.

CHESTNUT STUFFING FOR TURKEY

1 pound chestnuts	7 cups soft bread cubes
1½ cups chopped celery (with leaves)	2 teaspoons salt
	1½ teaspoons dried sage leaves
¾ cup finely chopped onion	1 teaspoon dried thyme leaves
1 cup butter or margarine	½ teaspoon pepper

Cut an X on rounded side of each chestnut. Heat chestnuts and enough water to cover to boiling. Boil uncovered 10 minutes; drain. Remove shells and skins. Heat chestnuts and enough water to cover to boiling. Boil uncovered 10 minutes; drain and chop.

Cook and stir celery, onion and butter in 10-inch skillet until onion is tender. Stir in about ⅓ of the bread cubes. Turn mixture into deep bowl. Add remaining bread cubes, the salt, sage, thyme, pepper and chestnuts; toss lightly. Stuff and roast turkey as described above. 9 CUPS STUFFING (ENOUGH FOR 12-POUND TURKEY).

Corn Bread Stuffing: Omit chestnuts. Substitute 9 cups corn bread cubes for the soft bread cubes.

Oyster Stuffing: Omit chestnuts. Increase soft bread cubes to 8 cups and add 2 cans (8 ounces each) oysters, drained and chopped.

PHEASANT WITH WINE SAUCE

1 teaspoon salt
¼ teaspoon ground cloves
¼ teaspoon ground nutmeg
¼ teaspoon ground thyme
¼ teaspoon pepper
2 pheasants
4 slices bacon
1 teaspoon instant chicken
    bouillon

½ cup boiling water
1 cup dry red wine
2 tablespoons finely chopped
    onion
2 tablespoons snipped parsley
⅓ cup currant jelly

Heat oven to 350°. Mix salt, cloves, nutmeg, thyme and pepper; rub over outsides and in cavities of pheasants. Tie legs of each pheasant. Place breast sides up on rack in jelly roll pan, 15½x10½x1 inch; place bacon slices over pheasant breasts. Stir bouillon into boiling water. Mix chicken bouillon, wine, onion and parsley; pour into pan. Bake uncovered until pheasants are tender, 1 to 1½ hours. Place pheasants on warm platter. Strain liquid into saucepan; add jelly. Heat until jelly is melted, stirring constantly. Cut pheasants into serving pieces; top with sauce. Nice served with wild rice.   4 TO 6 SERVINGS.

To Americans, all the birds of the air have been fair game at one time or another. From the wild turkey of the Pilgrims' days to the domesticated duck of today, the distinctive flavor of game birds has always lent itself beautifully to our methods of cooking.

SAVORY DUCKLING

1 ready-to-cook duckling (4 to 5
    pounds)
2 teaspoons salt
1 small onion
3 sprigs parsley

½ cup dry vermouth
½ cup dark corn syrup
1 tablespoon lemon juice
1 teaspoon ground coriander

Sprinkle cavity of duckling with salt; place onion and parsley in cavity. Fasten neck skin to back with skewers. Lift wing tips up and over back for natural brace. Place duckling breast side up on rack in shallow roasting pan.

Heat vermouth, corn syrup, lemon juice and coriander to boiling; reduce heat. Simmer uncovered, stirring occasionally, until reduced to ½ cup. Spoon ¼ cup of the sauce into cavity of duckling. Do not cover. Roast in 325° oven, pricking skin with fork and brushing occasionally with remaining sauce, until drumstick meat feels very soft, about 2½ hours. Place a piece of aluminum foil loosely over breast if duckling becomes too brown.   2 OR 3 SERVINGS.

BOSTON BAKED BEANS

2 pounds dried navy or pea
   beans (about 4 cups)
8 cups water
1 medium onion
½-pound piece salt pork (with
   rind)

1 cup molasses
3 tablespoons packed brown
   sugar
2 teaspoons salt
1½ teaspoons dry mustard
¼ teaspoon pepper

Heat beans and water to boiling in 3- to 4-quart Dutch oven; boil 2 minutes. Remove from heat; cover and let stand 1 hour.

Add enough water, if necessary, to cover beans. Heat to boiling; reduce heat. Cover and simmer until tender, 1 to 1½ hours. (To test, blow on a few beans in a spoon; skins will burst and peel back if done.) Drain beans, reserving liquid.

Heat oven to 300°. Place onion in ungreased 3- to 4-quart bean pot, casserole or Dutch oven; cover with beans. Cover pork with boiling water; let stand 5 minutes. Drain pork; cut through rind in crisscross pattern to depth of 1 inch. Bury pork rind side up in beans so that only rind shows. Mix molasses, sugar, salt, mustard, pepper and reserved bean liquid; pour over beans. Cover and bake 2½ to 3 hours. Uncover and bake 30 minutes. Add enough hot water during baking, if necessary, to keep beans moist.   12 TO 15 SERVINGS.

SOUTHERN BAKED BEANS

1 pound dried white marrow or
   navy beans (about 2 cups)
6 cups water
¾ pound lean salt pork or
   smoked pork, sliced
½ cup chopped onion
2 cloves garlic, finely chopped
½ teaspoon red pepper sauce
1 bay leaf, crumbled

¼ cup catsup
¼ cup molasses
1½ teaspoons dry mustard
½ teaspoon salt
½ teaspoon ground ginger
1½ teaspoons Worcestershire
   sauce
⅓ cup packed dark brown sugar

Heat beans and water to boiling; boil 2 minutes. Remove from heat; cover and let stand 1 hour. Stir in pork, onion, garlic, pepper sauce and bay leaf. Heat to boiling; reduce heat. Cover and simmer until beans are tender, 1½ to 2 hours. (Do not boil or beans will burst.)

Heat oven to 400°. Drain beans, reserving liquid. Add enough water, if necessary, to measure 2 cups. Stir catsup, molasses, mustard, salt, ginger and Worcestershire sauce into bean liquid. Place beans in ungreased shallow 2-quart casserole; pour reserved bean liquid over beans. Arrange pork slices on top; sprinkle with sugar. Bake uncovered 1 hour.   6 SERVINGS.

Pictured opposite.
Try an old New England twosome for a Saturday night menu: Boston Baked Beans (this page) and Boston Brown Bread (page 12).

SKILLET SPECIALTIES

RED FLANNEL HASH

1½ cups chopped cooked beef
   corned brisket*
1½ cups chopped cooked
   potatoes
1 can (16 ounces) diced beets,
   drained (1½ cups)

⅓ cup chopped onion
½ teaspoon salt
¼ teaspoon pepper
¼ cup shortening
Snipped parsley

Mix all ingredients except shortening and parsley. Heat shortening in 10-inch skillet over medium heat until melted. Spread beef mixture in skillet. Brown, turning occasionally with wide spatula, 10 to 15 minutes. Sprinkle with parsley. 4 SERVINGS.

*1 can (12 ounces) corned beef yields approximately 2 cups.

SLOPPY JOES

1 pound ground beef
½ cup chopped onion
⅓ cup chopped celery
⅓ cup chopped green pepper
⅓ cup catsup
¼ cup water

1 tablespoon Worcestershire
   sauce
⅛ teaspoon red pepper sauce
1 teaspoon salt
6 hamburger buns, split and
   toasted

Cook and stir ground beef and onion in 10-inch skillet until beef is brown and onion is tender; drain off fat. Stir in remaining ingredients except buns. Cover and cook over low heat just until vegetables are tender, 10 to 15 minutes. Fill buns with beef mixture. 6 SANDWICHES.

NOTE: For saucier Sloppy Joes, increase catsup to ½ cup.

LIVER AND ONIONS

2 medium onions, thinly sliced
3 tablespoons butter or
   margarine
1 pound beef liver, ½ to ¾ inch
   thick

½ cup all-purpose flour
¼ cup shortening
Salt
Pepper

Cook and stir onions and butter in 10-inch skillet until tender. Remove from skillet; keep warm. Coat liver with flour. Heat shortening in skillet. Cook liver in hot shortening over medium heat on each side until brown, 2 to 3 minutes. Add onions; heat until hot. Sprinkle with salt and pepper. 4 SERVINGS.

For early settlers and present-day campers and outdoorsmen alike, the skillet has been an essential cooking tool.

LAMB AND RED NOODLES

2 pounds lamb arm or blade chops or neck slices, ¾ inch thick
2 tablespoons water
3 cups water
1 can (6 ounces) tomato paste
1½ teaspoons salt
⅛ teaspoon pepper
Dash of cayenne red pepper
1 bay leaf, crumbled
1 large clove garlic, finely chopped
4 ounces uncooked wide egg noodles
½ cup shredded Cheddar cheese

Brown lamb chops in 10-inch skillet; drain off fat. Add 2 tablespoons water. Cover and simmer until lamb is tender, about 1 hour. Cool; remove lamb from bones.

Return lamb to skillet. Stir in 3 cups water, the tomato paste, salt, pepper, red pepper, bay leaf and garlic. Heat to boiling; reduce heat. Cover and simmer 30 minutes.

Stir in noodles. Cover and cook until noodles are tender, about 12 minutes. Sprinkle with cheese.   4 SERVINGS.

SPICY BRAISED VENISON

3- to 3½-pound venison chuck roast
2 onions, sliced
12 peppercorns
12 juniper berries (optional)
6 whole cloves
2 bay leaves
2 teaspoons salt
1½ cups red wine vinegar
1 cup boiling water
2 tablespoons shortening
½ cup cold water
¼ cup all-purpose flour
2 teaspoons sugar

Place venison roast, onions, peppercorns, juniper berries, cloves, bay leaves, salt, vinegar and 1 cup boiling water in earthenware bowl or glass baking dish. Cover with plastic wrap. Refrigerate at least 3 days, turning venison twice a day with 2 wooden spoons. (Never pierce venison with fork.)

Drain venison, reserving vinegar mixture. Heat shortening in 12-inch skillet or 4-quart Dutch oven; brown venison. Add vinegar mixture. Cover and simmer until venison is tender, 3 to 3½ hours. Remove venison and onions from skillet; keep warm. Strain and measure liquid in skillet. Add water, if necessary, to measure 2 cups; pour into skillet. Cover and simmer 10 minutes. Shake ½ cup cold water, the flour and sugar in tightly covered jar. Stir slowly into liquid in skillet. Heat to boiling, stirring constantly. Boil and stir 1 minute. Serve with venison and onions.   6 SERVINGS.

SMOTHERED RABBIT

2 domestic rabbits (2 to 2½
   pounds each) or 4 wild
   rabbits, cut up
1½ cups cider vinegar
½ cup chopped onion
2 tablespoons packed light
   brown sugar
1 tablespoon dry mustard
2 teaspoons salt

1 cup all-purpose flour
1 tablespoon granulated sugar
½ teaspoon pepper
¼ teaspoon grated nutmeg
Vegetable oil, lard, shortening
   or bacon fat
½ cup all-purpose flour
3 cups water

Place rabbit in shallow glass dish. Mix vinegar, onion, brown sugar, mustard and salt; pour over rabbit. Cover and refrigerate at least 12 hours but no longer than 24 hours, turning rabbit occasionally.

Drain rabbit and pat dry. Mix 1 cup flour, the granulated sugar, pepper and nutmeg. Coat rabbit with flour mixture. Heat oil ¼ inch deep in heavy 12-inch skillet. Brown rabbit; remove from skillet. Drain oil, reserving ½ cup. Stir in ½ cup flour; stir in water slowly. Heat to boiling, stirring constantly. Boil and stir 1 minute. Place rabbit in gravy; reduce heat. Cover and simmer until tender, 1 to 1½ hours. Stir in additional water if necessary.   4 TO 6 SERVINGS.

JAMBALAYA

2 medium onions, chopped
½ medium green pepper,
   chopped
1 clove garlic, finely chopped
3 tablespoons olive or vegetable
   oil
1 pound fresh or frozen raw
   shrimp, peeled and deveined
1 cup uncooked regular rice

2 cups chicken broth
1 can (16 ounces) tomatoes
1 teaspoon salt
⅛ teaspoon pepper
⅛ teaspoon ground thyme
⅛ teaspoon red pepper sauce
1 bay leaf, crumbled
½ pound cubed cooked ham
   (about 1½ cups)

Cook and stir onions, green pepper, garlic and 2 tablespoons of the oil in 4-quart Dutch oven over low heat 3 minutes. Add shrimp. Cook, stirring frequently, until shrimp are pink, about 5 minutes. Turn shrimp mixture into bowl; reserve.

Cook remaining 1 tablespoon oil and the rice in Dutch oven over medium-high heat, stirring frequently, until rice is light brown, about 10 minutes. Stir in chicken broth, tomatoes (with liquid), salt, pepper, thyme, pepper sauce and bay leaf. Heat to boiling; reduce heat. Cover and simmer until rice is tender, about 15 minutes. Stir in reserved shrimp mixture and the ham. Cover and cook just until shrimp and ham are hot.   6 SERVINGS.

BACON-FRIED CHICKEN

½ cup all-purpose flour
1 teaspoon salt
¼ teaspoon pepper
2½- to 3-pound broiler-fryer
    chicken, cut up

¼ pound bacon, cut into small
    pieces

Mix flour, salt and pepper. Coat chicken with flour mixture. Fry bacon partially in 10-inch skillet. Cook chicken and bacon over medium heat until chicken is brown, 15 to 20 minutes; reduce heat.

Cover tightly and simmer, turning chicken once or twice, until thickest pieces are done, 20 to 30 minutes. (If skillet cannot be covered tightly, add 1 to 2 tablespoons water.) Uncover and cook 10 minutes. 4 SERVINGS.

PHILADELPHIA SCRAPPLE

1¼ pounds pork blade steaks
2½ cups water
1½ teaspoons salt
¼ teaspoon pepper
½ cup yellow cornmeal

¼ cup all-purpose flour
½ teaspoon rubbed sage
¼ teaspoon ground allspice
Flour
1 tablespoon shortening

Heat pork steaks, water, salt and pepper to boiling in 2-quart saucepan; reduce heat. Cover and simmer until pork falls off bones, about 1½ hours.

Strain broth; refrigerate until cold. Cut pork into small pieces. Remove fat from broth. Mix cornmeal, ¼ cup flour, the sage and allspice in 2-quart saucepan. Stir in 1 cup of the broth. Cook over medium heat, stirring constantly, until mixture thickens. Stir in pork. Add enough water to remaining broth to measure 1½ cups; stir gradually into cornmeal mixture. Heat to boiling; reduce heat. Simmer uncovered 30 minutes. Spread evenly in greased loaf pan, 9x5x3 inches. Cover and refrigerate until firm, at least 12 hours. (Scrapple can be refrigerated at this point up to 36 hours longer. Wrap securely in aluminum foil.)

Unmold scrapple; cut into ½-inch slices. Coat with flour. Heat shortening in skillet. Brown slices on both sides in hot shortening. 8 SERVINGS (2 SLICES EACH).

Pennsylvania Scrapple: Substitute 1¼ pounds pork liver, kidney, heart and pork scraps for the pork blade steaks. Stir in 1 medium onion, chopped, with the pork.

The country skill of raising and curing pork to have a specific flavor is an old one, highly developed in Poland, Germany and Italy, where the ability to control ham's flavor has long been practiced. In Italy, for example, the characteristic flavor of prosciutto comes from feeding the pigs on the whey from Parmesan cheese. Many aspects of American curing methods came from such Old World knowledge, but others were discovered by accident.

Near Smithfield, Virginia, farmers noticed that the meat from pigs that grazed on peanuts had a special taste. Gradually the farmers learned curing techniques that heightened that special flavor, and the name *Smithfield* on ham became an assurance of excellence. Only ham cured in or immediately around the town of Smithfield can bear that name. These noble hams, festooned with a string of cranberries, share the center of attraction with the turkey at Thanksgiving and other holiday feasts in the South.

For less auspicious occasions, country hams are popular in every nook and cranny of America. Because of the salt used in the curing process, Smithfield and country ham should be trimmed and soaked in warm water before cooking. In Tennessee, Kentucky and the Midwest, where country ham curing is still an art, Fried Ham and Red-Eye Gravy, a breakfast classic, has never gone out of style.

FRIED HAM AND RED-EYE GRAVY

2 packages (12 ounces each)
    country ham slices

1 cup hot coffee or water
Dixie Biscuits (page 10)

Trim excess fat from ham slices; reserve. Soak ham in warm water 15 minutes; drain. Heat reserved ham fat in 10-inch skillet over medium heat until melted. Brown ham on both sides over medium heat; remove to warm platter. Pour drippings from skillet. Pour hot coffee into skillet. Stir and scrape ham particles from skillet; pour over Dixie Biscuits. Serve with ham.   4 TO 6 SERVINGS.

CORN-EGG SCRAMBLE

½ pound bacon, cut into small
    pieces
4 eggs
1 can (16 ounces) whole kernel
    corn, drained

Salt
Pepper

Fry bacon in 10-inch skillet until crisp; drain off fat. Beat eggs; stir in corn. Pour over bacon pieces in skillet. Cook and stir until eggs are thickened throughout but still moist. Season with salt and pepper. 4 SERVINGS.

Pictured opposite.
Country ham is no stranger to a hearty farmland breakfast—shown here in Fried Ham and Red-Eye Gravy (this page). Serve it with Corn-Egg Scramble (this page), Dixie Biscuits (page 10) and Peach Honey (page 122).

Cod is a dreary name that hides this fish's virtuoso talents. In the Northeast, generations of Americans have been raised on Codfish Cakes, Codfish Puff and other salted-cod recipes. Most New England households kept a barrel of cod in the cellar, along with the root vegetables. And in Boston, there's even a plaque in the government chambers commemorating this favorite fish.

CODFISH PUFF

½ pound boneless salt cod	1 tablespoon butter or
3 medium potatoes, pared and	margarine
cut into ½-inch cubes (2½	⅛ teaspoon pepper
cups)	2 tablespoons shortening or
1½ cups hot water	bacon fat
4 eggs, beaten	Catsup or cheese sauce

Place cod in bowl; cover with cold water. Soak 1 to 2 hours; drain. Repeat process.

Place cod and potatoes in 3-quart saucepan; cover with hot water. Heat to boiling. Cover and cook until potatoes are tender, about 20 minutes. Mash or beat undrained cod and potatoes 1 to 2 minutes on medium speed in large mixer bowl until smooth. Beat in eggs, butter and pepper.

Heat shortening in 10-inch skillet until melted. Spread cod mixture evenly in skillet. Cover and cook over low heat until golden brown crust forms on bottom and side, about 10 minutes. Invert on heat-proof platter. Serve with catsup.   6 SERVINGS.

DEEP FRIES

CODFISH CAKES

4 ounces boneless salt cod	⅓ cup finely chopped onion
5 or 6 medium potatoes, pared	2 tablespoons flour
and cut into ¼-inch cubes	⅛ teaspoon pepper
(about 4 cups)	Catsup

Place cod in bowl; cover with cold water. Soak 1 to 2 hours; drain.

Place cod, potatoes and onion in 3-quart saucepan; cover with hot water. Heat to boiling. Cover and cook until potatoes are tender, about 20 minutes; drain. Mash or beat potato mixture about 1 minute on high speed in large mixer bowl until smooth. Stir in flour and pepper. Refrigerate until cold, about 1 hour.

Heat vegetable oil or shortening (3 to 4 inches) to 375° in deep fat fryer or heavy saucepan. Drop potato mixture by rounded table-spoonfuls, 4 or 5 at a time, into hot oil. Fry until golden brown, about 2 minutes; drain. Serve with catsup.   4 SERVINGS.

In American kitchens, "fried" has become a natural adjective for chicken. But the method of frying varies from cook to cook. Some prefer deep fat, others shallow fat. Some prefer a batter coating, others bread crumbs or flour.

When you fry chicken—or other fare—in deep fat, the temperature of the oil is the key to success. Use a deep-fat thermometer to determine exactly when the oil reaches the correct temperature.

CHICKEN WITH PUFFITS AND MILK GRAVY

2½- to 3-pound broiler-fryer chicken, cut up	Puffits (below)
	2 tablespoons flour
½ cup all-purpose flour*	½ teaspoon salt
1 teaspoon salt	1½ cups milk
¼ teaspoon pepper	

Remove any excess fat from chicken. Place chicken in 3-quart saucepan. Add enough water to cover. Heat to boiling; reduce heat. Cover and simmer 20 minutes. Drain chicken and pat dry.

Heat vegetable oil or shortening (3 to 4 inches) to 360° in deep fat fryer or heavy saucepan. Mix ½ cup flour, 1 teaspoon salt and the pepper. Coat chicken with flour mixture. Fry in hot oil until golden, about 6 minutes; drain on paper towels.

Increase oil temperature to 375°. Slide Puffits carefully into hot oil, turning as they rise to surface. Fry until golden brown, about 8 minutes; drain on paper towels. Keep chicken and Puffits warm in oven while preparing gravy.

Blend 2 tablespoons of the hot cooking oil, 2 tablespoons flour and ½ teaspoon salt in 1-quart saucepan. Cook over low heat, stirring constantly, until mixture is smooth and bubbly. Remove from heat; stir in milk gradually. Heat to boiling, stirring constantly. Boil and stir 1 minute. Serve with chicken and Puffits.   4 SERVINGS.

*If using self-rising flour, decrease salt to ½ teaspoon.

PUFFITS

1½ cups all-purpose flour**	¼ cup shortening
1½ teaspoons baking powder	½ cup milk
1 teaspoon salt	

Mix flour, baking powder and salt. Cut in shortening until mixture looks like fine crumbs. Stir in almost all the milk. Stir in just enough additional milk to make a soft, puffy, easy-to-roll dough. (Too much milk makes dough sticky, not enough makes Puffits dry.) Round up dough on lightly floured cloth-covered board. Roll ½ inch thick. Cut with floured 2-inch biscuit cutter.

**If using self-rising flour, omit baking powder and salt.

CORN DOGS

1 pound frankfurters	3 tablespoons shortening
1 cup all-purpose flour*	¾ cup milk
2 tablespoons cornmeal	1 egg, beaten
1½ teaspoons baking powder	1 medium onion, grated
½ teaspoon salt	(optional)

Pat frankfurters dry with paper towels. Heat vegetable oil or shortening (3 to 4 inches) to 365° in deep fat fryer or heavy saucepan. Mix flour, cornmeal, baking powder and salt. Cut in shortening. Stir in milk, egg and onion. Dip frankfurters into batter, allowing excess batter to drip into bowl. Fry in hot oil, turning once, until brown, about 6 minutes; drain on paper towels. Insert wooden skewer in end of each frankfurter if desired.   5 SERVINGS.

*If using self-rising flour, omit baking powder and salt.

MARYLAND CRAB CAKES

1 pound Atlantic crabmeat, drained and cartilage removed	½ teaspoon salt
	⅛ teaspoon pepper
	2 tablespoons butter or margarine, melted
1½ cups soft white bread crumbs (no crusts)	
	2 egg yolks, beaten
1 teaspoon dry mustard	

Mix all ingredients. Shape into 4 patties 3½ inches in diameter and about ¾ inch thick. Refrigerate until firm, about 1½ hours.

Heat vegetable oil or shortening (1 inch) to 375°. Fry patties until golden brown on both sides, 4 to 5 minutes; drain.   4 PATTIES.

CLAM FRITTERS

¾ cup all-purpose flour	2 cans (8 ounces each) minced clams,* drained (reserve ¼ cup liquid)
1 teaspoon baking powder	
½ teaspoon salt	
¼ cup milk	Cocktail sauce or tartar sauce
1 egg	

Heat vegetable oil or shortening (3 to 4 inches) to 375° in deep fat fryer or heavy saucepan. Beat flour, baking powder, salt, milk, egg and reserved clam liquid with hand beater until smooth. Stir in clams. Drop by level tablespoonfuls into hot oil. Fry until golden brown, about 5 minutes; drain on paper towels. Serve with cocktail sauce.   3 OR 4 SERVINGS.

*1 cup shucked fresh clams, finely chopped, can be substituted for the canned clams.

Pictured opposite.
Whether your produce is homegrown or store-bought, you'll enjoy these fresh ways to serve it. Clockwise from top: Stewed Plums (page 116), Pecan Eggplant (page 100), Broccoli with Easy Cheese Sauce (page 96), Mashed Potatoes and Rutabaga (page 104) and Caesar Salad (page 108).

KITCHEN GARDEN

KITCHEN GARDEN

Throngs of people stop at roadside fruit and vegetable stands on summer weekends. The sight of deep-red tomatoes, potatoes with dirt still on the skins, crisp peas and just-picked peaches is immensely satisfying, particularly if the stand happens to be on the edge of an orchard or a field of tall green corn.

So appealing are these fresh foods to Americans that in recent years more and more people are planting their own. This revival of kitchen gardens, or Victory gardens as they were called during World War II, may take form as a small plot in the backyard, a few flowerpots of cherry tomatoes or herbs on the windowsill or half an acre in the country. Whatever the circumstances, the impulse is the same: to return to a natural connection with the growing of our food.

Satisfying as it is to raise your own fruits and vegetables or to buy directly from farmers by the road, the supermarket produce available to most of us is, in fact, not only fresh but of an astonishing diversity. We are spoiled enough now to regard broccoli, beans, peppers, eggplant and many other vegetables as year-round crops. Fruits our ancestors would have stared at in amazement, such as pineapples, tangerines and dates, seem quite ordinary.

Many early settlers, however, survived on the native crops that they were able to store for the winter and plants that they could gather in the wilds. For them the first vegetable of spring was often the dandelion. Although most people now see dandelions only as the scourge of lawns, to our ancestors it was useful as a vegetable, salad, soup, tea and even as a wine. Many neglected plants that were eaten in early America are still abundant in the woods today.

It seems that practically everyone who ever immigrated to America felt compelled to describe its natural bounty in diaries and letters. Edmund Flagg, writing of Illinois in 1837, was amazed at the fruits: "Endless thickets of the wild plum and the blackberry, interlaced and matted together by the young grape-vines streaming with gorgeous clusters, were to be seen stretching for miles along the plain. . . . Vast groves of the ruby crab-apple, the golden persimmon, the black and white mulberry, and the wild cherry, were sprinkled with their rainbow hues in isolated masses over the prairie."

That wealth of fruit is still available, though now it is more apt to be from carefully controlled cultivation than from wild thickets and clusters stretching along the prairie. Seven thousand varieties of apples grow in the United States today. Some types are available all year, along with many citrus fruits. Even the perishable peaches, pears, grapes and plums are longer seasonal crops now. Until the turn of the century, grapefruit was almost unknown outside Florida, and there was no commercial cultivation of melons at all. Judging from the number of times watermelons are mentioned in connection with nineteenth-century picnics in old diaries, everyone must have had their own backyard patch. Mark Twain appreciated them so much that he insisted Eve never would have repented if she'd tasted a watermelon instead of an apple.

Choose among America's year-round diversity of produce for traditional or new recipes alike.

The widespread distribution of America's natural wealth of produce is, of course, quite recent. What was available to most cooks was the long-lasting produce they were able to winter over or dry: root vegetables, beans, apples and, primarily, corn. The storage of these was usually in the cellar of the house or in an outdoor root cellar dug out of the side of a hill and faced with stones. Even in the wake of the almost unlimited choice we enjoy all year, these winter vegetables retain their popularity in our cuisine. We've gathered recipes that treat these favorites imaginatively: our Maple Baked Acorn Squash is beautifully glazed with syrup, our Sweet Potato Chips are a variation of an all-time favorite. We've also included recipes for less familiar vegetables, such as Creamed Radishes and Parsnip Cakes, because they're so good they deserve a comeback.

Perhaps it is because American cooks were used to preparing root vegetables and reconstituting dried fruits that led them to overcook the more tender vegetables when they were available. In 1837, Eliza Leslie's cookbook advises us to boil a cabbage or cauliflower two hours! Today we prefer the crisp texture and peak flavor vegetables keep if cooking time is brief and the pot is taken immediately off the burner, not left on for the vegetables to wilt and lose their color and vitamins while being kept warm.

In addition to simplicity of basic preparation, a special plus for vegetable cookery in inflationary times is its economy. Many of us coping with the high prices of meat are discovering that entire dinners of vegetable combinations can be satisfying and creative.

Reading old cookbooks, one almost can hear the homilies of the last centuries: "Waste not, want not," and "A penny saved. . . ." The household art that did just that was preserving. "Putting up" fruits and vegetables was another important way to be thrifty and to outwit winter. Today, as in the last century, a bumper crop in the garden is likely to go straight to the pantry shelf, or its modern equivalent. The jewel-colored rows of tomatoes, peppers, peaches and berries were once counted on to brighten the table on drab January days. Now, long after that need is gone, preserving still is popular. Both improved techniques and more time to enjoy cooking have contributed to this new interest in the traditional art. Part of its pleasure might also be in fulfilling those early notions of thrift, such as making Watermelon Rind Pickles or gathering in all the still-green tomatoes before the first frost for a tangy Green Tomato Mincemeat. But the abiding interest, old and new, must come from the very particular satisfaction of serving or giving your own Spiced Pickled Peaches, Dilled Beans or Apple Butter. Despite the many excellent products available commercially, *your* brand of Bread-and-Butter Pickles somehow seems a little crisper, *your* Mincemeat a little more special.

This pantry shelf and our harvest of fruits and vegetables is the best of home-grown America, in touch with its past but authentically America today.

VEGETABLES

GREEN BEANS, CAPE COD STYLE

1 pound green beans, cut in
  halves lengthwise
2 tablespoons cream
¼ teaspoon salt

1 tablespoon butter or
  margarine
Dash of pepper

Heat beans and 1 inch salted water (½ teaspoon salt to 1 cup water) to boiling. Cook uncovered 5 minutes. Cover and cook until tender, 10 to 15 minutes; drain. Stir in remaining ingredients.   4 SERVINGS.

THREE-BEAN CASSEROLE

1 package (10 ounces) frozen
  lima beans
1 package (9 ounces) frozen cut
  green beans
1 package (9 ounces) frozen cut
  wax beans
2 tablespoons butter or
  margarine

2 tablespoons flour
¾ teaspoon salt
½ teaspoon monosodium
  glutamate
⅛ teaspoon pepper
1 cup milk
½ cup grated Parmesan or
  Romano cheese

Cook beans as directed on packages except—omit salt; drain. (If beans have the same cooking time, they can be cooked together.) Place in ungreased baking dish, 8x8x2 inches.

Heat oven to 375°. Heat butter in 2-quart saucepan over low heat until melted. Stir in flour, salt, monosodium glutamate and pepper. Cook, stirring constantly, until mixture is smooth and bubbly. Remove from heat; stir in milk. Heat to boiling, stirring constantly. Boil and stir 1 minute. Pour over beans. Sprinkle with cheese. Bake uncovered until bubbly and brown, about 20 minutes.   8 SERVINGS.

TEXAS PINTO BEANS

1 pound dried pinto beans
  (about 2 cups)
4 cups water
¼-pound piece salt pork (with
  rind)

2 teaspoons chili powder
¼ teaspoon red pepper sauce

Heat beans and water to boiling in 3-quart saucepan; boil 2 minutes. Remove from heat; cover and let stand 1 hour.

Stir in pork, chili powder and pepper sauce. Heat to boiling; reduce heat. Cover and simmer until beans are tender, about 1½ hours. Remove pork; slice and stir into beans.   12 SERVINGS.

RED BEANS AND RICE

1 pound dried red, pinto or
    kidney beans (about 2 cups)
4 cups water
¼ pound lean salt pork or
    smoked pork, cut up

1 cup chopped onion
1 tablespoon flour
1 teaspoon salt
½ teaspoon red pepper sauce
4 cups hot cooked rice

Heat beans and water to boiling in 3-quart saucepan; boil 2 minutes. Remove from heat; cover and let stand 1 hour.

Brown pork in 8-inch skillet. Add onion and flour; cook and stir until onion is tender. Stir pork mixture, salt and pepper sauce into beans. Heat to boiling; reduce heat. Cover and simmer, stirring occasionally, until beans are tender, 1½ to 2 hours. Add enough water, if necessary, to prevent sticking. Serve over rice.   8 SERVINGS.

In some parts of the South it is fervently believed that black-eyed peas for dinner on New Year's Day will bring good luck all year long. Consequently, black-eyed peas and hog jowl are often considered traditional fare on the first of January.

Also dear to the Southern heart, but with no such guarantee of good fortune, are Hoppin' John and Red Beans and Rice, the latter a spicy Creole dish.

HOPPIN' JOHN

½ pound dried black-eyed peas
    (about 1 cup)
3½ cups water
¼ pound slab bacon, lean salt
    pork or smoked pork
1 onion, sliced
¼ to ½ teaspoon very finely
    chopped fresh hot pepper or
    ⅛ to ¼ teaspoon crushed
    dried hot pepper

½ cup uncooked long-grain rice
1 teaspoon salt
Pepper

Heat peas and water to boiling in 2-quart saucepan; boil 2 minutes. Remove from heat; cover and let stand 1 hour.

Cut bacon into 8 pieces. Stir bacon, onion and hot pepper into peas. Heat to boiling; reduce heat. Cover and simmer until peas are tender, 1 to 1½ hours.

Stir in rice, salt and pepper. Cover and simmer, stirring occasionally, until rice is tender, about 25 minutes. Stir in additional water, if necessary, to cook rice.   6 TO 8 SERVINGS.

B roccoli, cauliflower and cabbage, all from the same family tree, are hardy vegetables that travel well. The irrigated farmlands of the West now keep us stocked with a fresh supply all year. Although these are not native plants, even the earliest cookbooks describe how to prepare them. One advises that if care is taken in cooking, cabbage can retain its beauty. This, of course, is every bit as true today. Similarly, both broccoli and cauliflower can benefit from a little special care.

BROCCOLI WITH EASY CHEESE SAUCE

1½ pounds broccoli
6 ounces process American
   cheese, sliced
⅓ cup milk

¼ teaspoon onion salt
1 drop red pepper sauce
   (optional)

Heat 1 inch salted water (½ teaspoon salt to 1 cup water) to boiling. Add broccoli. Cover and heat to boiling. Cook until stems are tender, 12 to 15 minutes; drain.

Heat remaining ingredients over medium heat, stirring frequently, until cheese is melted and mixture is smooth, 6 to 8 minutes. Pour cheese sauce over broccoli.   4 SERVINGS.

G reen or red cabbage, Savoy cabbage, Danish or Chinese cabbage—some of the several hundred varieties of this versatile vegetable grow in every state and every climate. In Alaska, the vegetable growing season is limited to a few weeks in summer when the sun shines for twenty hours a day. This short but intensive concentration causes cabbages there to grow up to sixty pounds each.

QUICK CRISPY CABBAGE

1 medium head green cabbage
   (about 1½ pounds), shredded
½ cup milk
1 tablespoon butter or
   margarine

½ teaspoon salt
Dash of pepper

Heat cabbage and milk to simmering in 10-inch skillet over medium heat, stirring frequently. Cover and simmer, stirring occasionally, until cabbage is crisp-tender, about 5 minutes. Stir in butter, salt and pepper.   4 SERVINGS.

FRIED CABBAGE, COUNTRY STYLE

2 tablespoons bacon fat
1 medium head green cabbage
    (about 1½ pounds),
    shredded
2 tablespoons cream

1½ teaspoons lemon juice or
    vinegar
Salt
Pepper

Heat bacon fat in 10-inch skillet. Add cabbage. Cook over low heat, stirring frequently, until light brown. Cover and cook, stirring occasionally, until crisp-tender, about 5 minutes. Stir in cream and lemon juice; heat until cream is hot. Sprinkle with salt and pepper. 4 SERVINGS.

Fried Red Cabbage: Substitute vegetable oil for the bacon fat and red cabbage for the green cabbage.

CREAMY CAULIFLOWER SOUP

2 cups water
1 medium head cauliflower
    (about 2 pounds), broken
    into flowerets, or 6 cups
    cauliflowerets
¾ cup thinly sliced celery
½ cup chopped onion
1 tablespoon lemon juice
2 tablespoons butter or
    margarine

2 tablespoons flour
2½ cups water
1 tablespoon instant chicken
    bouillon
¾ teaspoon salt
⅛ teaspoon pepper
Dash of ground nutmeg
½ cup whipping cream
Grated cheese (optional)

It's always fun to shop at outdoor market stalls like this one, near Boston's Faneuil Hall.

Heat 2 cups water to boiling in 3-quart saucepan. Add cauliflower, celery, onion and lemon juice. Cover and heat to boiling. Cook until tender, about 10 minutes; do not drain. Press cauliflower mixture through food mill. (Or place in blender container. Cover and blend until uniform consistency.)

Heat butter in 3-quart saucepan over low heat until melted. Stir in flour. Cook, stirring constantly, until mixture is smooth and bubbly. Remove from heat; stir in 2½ cups water. Heat to boiling, stirring constantly. Boil and stir 1 minute. Stir in cauliflower mixture, bouillon, salt, pepper and nutmeg. Heat just to boiling. Stir in cream; heat but do not boil. Serve with grated cheese. 8 SERVINGS.

Creamy Broccoli Soup: Substitute 1½ pounds broccoli, cut up, for the cauliflower; omit the lemon juice.

Creamy Cabbage Soup: Substitute 1 medium head cabbage (about 1½ pounds), shredded, for the cauliflower; cook only 5 minutes.

A nineteenth-century etiquette book cautions, "It is not elegant to *gnaw* Indian corn." In spite of that, corn-on-the-cob always has been an American institution.

Corn was the great resource of the New World. By the time the colonists arrived, it already was a highly cultivated plant. The Indians, who had refined it from a wild grass, depended on corn as the staple of their diet, a complete food used as a grain, a vegetable and even as tobacco. In all the Indian languages, *corn* translates to "our life."

One of the first history lessons American children learn is how the Indians taught the Pilgrims to cultivate corn by planting the kernels in the soil with a small fish, as fertilizer, in each mound. The Pilgrims—and every other group of settlers—quickly learned to use all parts of the corn plant.

Misickquatash, which sounded like "succotash" to English ears, could be made all year from dried kernels and beans simmered in bear, venison or other fat. Later, Corn Oysters with maple syrup became popular for breakfast or, served plain, for supper. Skillet Corn offers a more genteel mode of eating corn, for those who don't want "to gnaw Indian corn."

CORN OYSTERS

1 cup bacon fat
1 cup vegetable oil
1 cup all-purpose flour
1 teaspoon baking powder
1 teaspoon salt

2 eggs, slightly beaten
1 can (16 ounces) whole kernel corn, drained (reserve ¼ cup liquid)

Heat fat and oil to 375° in 10-inch skillet. Mix flour, baking powder, salt, eggs and reserved corn liquid. Stir in corn. Drop by rounded tablespoonfuls into hot fat. Fry until golden brown on all sides, 4 to 5 minutes; drain on paper towels.   2 DOZEN CORN OYSTERS.

Nutmeg-Corn Oysters: Stir in 1 teaspoon ground nutmeg with the flour.

SKILLET CORN

4 ears corn
2 tablespoons butter or margarine
2 tablespoons light cream or milk

¼ teaspoon salt
Dash of pepper

Cut enough kernels from corn to measure 2 cups (scrape ears with back of knife to extract all pulp and milk). Cook and stir all ingredients in 10-inch skillet over medium heat until butter is melted. Cover and cook over low heat until corn is tender, 10 to 15 minutes.   3 OR 4 SERVINGS.

Pictured opposite.
Regional variations on a truly native food—corn. Clockwise from top: The South contributes Brunswick Stew (page 59); Skillet Corn (this page) and Summer Succotash (page 100) come from New England; and the Midwest gives us Corn Oysters (this page) and Corn Relish (page 129).

After the most frugal years had passed, the colonists cooked a succotash with chicken and corned beef, which they served every year on December 21, the anniversary of the Pilgrims' landing at Plymouth Rock.

The Summer Succotash below adds a lavish dash of cream to the original succotash's ingredients.

SUMMER SUCCOTASH

4 ears corn
2 cups shelled fresh lima beans
   (about 3 pounds unshelled)
⅓ cup cut-up lean salt pork or
   bacon

¼ cup chopped onion
½ cup light cream (20%)
¼ teaspoon salt
⅛ teaspoon pepper

Cut enough kernels from corn to measure 2 cups. Mix beans, pork and onion in 3-quart saucepan; add enough water to cover. Heat to boiling; reduce heat. Cover and simmer until beans are tender, 20 to 25 minutes. Stir in corn. Heat to boiling; reduce heat. Cover and simmer until corn is tender, about 5 minutes; drain. Stir in cream, salt and pepper. Heat until cream is hot, stirring occasionally.   6 SERVINGS.

Although eggplant has been settled in this country for a long time, it still has something of an exotic air about it, as though it had determined to keep its foreign citizenship. Many popular recipes for eggplant can be traced to Turkish, Greek or Italian origins by the use of olive oil, Parmesan cheese and other ingredients not indigenous to America. Pecan Eggplant, however, with its use of butter and pecans, is a native son.

PECAN EGGPLANT

¼ cup butter or margarine
1 medium eggplant (about 1½
   pounds), pared and cut into
   ½-inch slices
1 cup light cream (20%)

1 teaspoon salt
½ teaspoon paprika
⅛ teaspoon pepper
½ cup chopped pecans

Heat oven to 300°. Heat butter in 10-inch skillet over low heat until melted. Add eggplant. Cook, turning once, until golden brown. Place in ungreased baking dish, 13½x8¾x1¾ inches. Pour cream over eggplant. Sprinkle with salt, paprika, pepper and pecans. Bake uncovered until cream is absorbed, about 1 hour.   4 SERVINGS.

Okra and tomatoes have a natural affinity for each other. Both belong in burgoos, Brunswick stews and gumbos. Okra Skillet combines tomatoes, onion and corn with okra in a sort of vegetable gumbo, bounteous and colorful.

OKRA SKILLET

¼ cup finely cut-up lean salt
    pork (about ¼ pound)*
½ cup chopped onion
2 cups sliced okra (about ¾
    pound) or 1 package (10
    ounces) frozen cut okra,
    thawed

4 medium tomatoes, peeled
    and cut into eighths
1 cup fresh corn (2 to 3 ears)
Dash of pepper

Cook and stir pork and onion in 10-inch skillet until pork is golden; stir in okra. Cook over medium-high heat, stirring constantly, 3 minutes. Stir in tomatoes and corn. Cover and simmer until corn is tender, 10 to 15 minutes. Stir in pepper.   4 SERVINGS.

*2 tablespoons butter or margarine can be substituted for the pork; stir in 1 teaspoon salt with the pepper.

ORANGE BEETS

1¼ pounds beets (about 5
    medium)
6 cups water
1 tablespoon vinegar
1 teaspoon salt
1 tablespoon cornstarch
1 tablespoon packed brown
    sugar

¾ teaspoon salt
Dash of pepper
¾ cup orange juice
1 tablespoon vinegar
1 teaspoon finely shredded
    orange peel

Cut off all but 2 inches of beet tops; leave root ends attached. Heat water, 1 tablespoon vinegar and 1 teaspoon salt to boiling in 3-quart saucepan. Add beets. Cover and heat to boiling. Cook until beets are tender, 35 to 45 minutes; drain. Run cold water over beets; slip off skins and remove root ends. Cut beets into slices.

Mix cornstarch, sugar, ¾ teaspoon salt and the pepper in 1-quart saucepan. Stir orange juice and 1 tablespoon vinegar gradually into cornstarch mixture. Cook, stirring constantly, until mixture thickens and boils. Boil and stir 1 minute. Stir in beets and orange peel; heat until beets are hot.   4 SERVINGS.

FRIED PARSNIPS

1½ pounds parsnips (about 6 medium)
2 tablespoons butter or margarine

Freshly ground pepper

Heat 1 inch salted water (½ teaspoon salt to 1 cup water) to boiling. Add parsnips. Cover and heat to boiling. Cook until tender, 20 to 30 minutes; drain. Cut into ½-inch slices. Heat butter in 10-inch skillet over low heat until melted. Add parsnips. Cook, stirring frequently, until golden brown. (Add butter if necessary.) Sprinkle with pepper.   4 SERVINGS.

Digging up the potato is the first step in bringing this popular and versatile root vegetable to the market place.

When village houses with root cellars began to give way to apartments with central heating housed in the cellar, we lost touch with several delicious vegetables that used to winter over nicely in dark corners, along with the barrels of cider, salted fish and maple sugar.

Many of us have never tasted rutabagas, parsnips or turnips. Only the potato's popularity escaped from the root cellar undiminished. Perhaps its place in the American menu is due, in no small part, to the many Irish-Americans who still recall stories of the devastating potato famine that impelled their forbears to come to this country.

Root vegetables have a particular strength of character, an earthiness readily apparent in Fried Parsnips but only hinted at in Parsnip Cakes and in Mashed Potatoes and Rutabaga.

PARSNIP CAKES

1¼ pounds parsnips (about 5 medium)
2 tablespoons flour
½ teaspoon salt
Dash of pepper
2 tablespoons butter or margarine, softened

1 tablespoon chopped onion
1 egg, beaten
Dried bread crumbs or cracker crumbs
¼ cup shortening

Heat 1 inch salted water (½ teaspoon salt to 1 cup water) to boiling. Add parsnips. Cover and heat to boiling. Cook until tender, 20 to 30 minutes; drain and mash.

Mix parsnips, flour, salt, pepper, butter, onion and egg. Shape parsnip mixture into 8 patties; coat with crumbs. Heat shortening in 10-inch skillet over low heat. Add parsnip patties. Cook over medium heat, turning once, until golden brown, about 5 minutes. 4 SERVINGS.

The potato portion of today's meat-and-potato meals usually means "baked," "mashed" or "French fried." Good though these treatments are, the following recipes from yesteryear will add a welcome change of pace to that most American twosome.

OLD-TIMEY CREAMED POTATOES

5 or 6 medium potatoes, pared
    and cut into ¼-inch cubes
    (about 4 cups)
2 cups half-and-half

1 teaspoon salt
⅛ teaspoon pepper
Snipped parsley or chives

Heat potatoes, half-and-half, salt and pepper to simmering in heavy 10-inch skillet over low heat, stirring frequently. Cover and simmer, stirring frequently, until potatoes are tender, about 30 minutes. Sprinkle with parsley.   4 TO 6 SERVINGS.

PENNSYLVANIA POTATO FILLING

3 eggs
1½ cups mashed cooked
    potatoes
1½ cups milk
4 cups Italian or French bread
    cubes

½ cup chopped onion
¼ cup butter or margarine
1 teaspoon salt
⅛ teaspoon pepper

Heat oven to 375°. Beat eggs, potatoes and milk in large mixer bowl until smooth. Cook and stir bread cubes, onion and butter in 10-inch skillet until bread cubes are light brown and onion is tender. Stir bread cube mixture, salt and pepper into potato mixture. Turn into greased 1½-quart casserole. Bake uncovered until top is golden, about 1 hour.   6 TO 8 SERVINGS.

FARM-FRIED POTATOES

2 tablespoons shortening or
    vegetable oil
5 or 6 medium potatoes, pared
    and thinly sliced (about 4
    cups)

1 large onion, thinly sliced
1½ teaspoons salt
Pepper
2 tablespoons butter or
    margarine

Heat shortening in 10-inch skillet until melted. Layer ⅓ each of potato and onion slices in skillet; sprinkle each layer with ½ teaspoon salt and dash of pepper. Dot top layer with butter. Cover and cook over medium heat 20 minutes. Uncover and cook until potatoes are brown, turning once.   4 TO 6 SERVINGS.

MASHED POTATOES AND RUTABAGA

3 medium potatoes, pared and
   cut up (about 2 cups)
1 large rutabaga (about 2
   pounds), pared and cut into
   ½-inch cubes

1 teaspoon sugar
3 tablespoons butter or
   margarine
1 teaspoon salt
⅛ teaspoon pepper

Heat 1 inch salted water (½ teaspoon salt to 1 cup water) to boiling
in each of 2 saucepans. Add potatoes to one saucepan and rutabaga
and sugar to the other saucepan. Cover and heat to boiling. Cook
until potatoes and rutabaga are tender, 20 to 25 minutes; drain.
Mash potatoes and rutabaga together until no lumps remain. Beat in
butter, salt and pepper until mixture is smooth and fluffy. (Beat in
enough hot milk, if necessary, to make mixture smooth and
fluffy.)　6 SERVINGS.

CREAMED RADISHES

1⅓ pounds red radishes, thinly
   sliced (about 4 cups)
2 tablespoons butter or
   margarine

2 tablespoons flour
1 teaspoon salt
⅛ teaspoon pepper
½ cup whipping cream

Place radishes in 3-quart saucepan; add enough water to cover. Heat
to boiling; reduce heat. Simmer uncovered until crisp-tender, 5 to 7
minutes; drain, reserving 1 cup liquid. Return radishes to saucepan.

Heat butter in 1-quart saucepan over low heat until melted. Stir in
flour, salt and pepper. Cook, stirring constantly, until mixture is
smooth and bubbly. Remove from heat; stir in cream and reserved
radish liquid. Heat to boiling, stirring constantly. Boil and stir 1
minute. Stir into radishes; heat until radishes are hot. Sprinkle with
snipped parsley or chives if desired.　6 TO 8 SERVINGS.

MAPLE BAKED ACORN SQUASH

2 acorn squash (1 to 1½ pounds
   each)
4 tablespoons maple-flavored
   or maple syrup

4 tablespoons cream

Heat oven to 350°. Cut each squash in half; remove seeds and fibers.
Place squash cut sides up in ungreased baking pan. Spoon 1 tablespoon syrup and 1 tablespoon cream into each half. Bake uncovered
until tender, about 1 hour.　4 SERVINGS.

Do you know the difference between yams and sweet potatoes? Although used interchangeably in cooking, they are not related botanically. Sweet potatoes are members of the morning glory family. Their skin and flesh are paler and somewhat drier than the darker orange yam's. Yams are noticeably sweeter than sweet potatoes.

Like pumpkin, both sweet potatoes and yams blend well with other flavors. Because of this they are prepared as muffins and sweet pies and as vegetables with many variations, such as the spice and fruit ones following Candied Sweet Potatoes or Yams. Deep-fried Sweet Potato Chips are a novel accompaniment for pork roasts and hams.

CANDIED SWEET POTATOES OR YAMS

2 pounds sweet potatoes or yams (about 6 medium) or 1 can (23 ounces) sweet potatoes or yams, drained
½ cup packed brown sugar

3 tablespoons butter or margarine
3 tablespoons water
½ teaspoon salt

If using fresh sweet potatoes or yams, heat enough salted water to cover potatoes (½ teaspoon salt to 1 cup water) to boiling. Add potatoes. Cover and heat to boiling. Cook until tender, 30 to 35 minutes; drain. Slip off skins. Cut potatoes into ½-inch slices. If using canned potatoes, cut into ½-inch slices.

Heat sugar, butter, water and salt in 8-inch skillet over medium heat, stirring constantly, until smooth and bubbly. Add potato slices; stir gently until slices are glazed and hot.   4 TO 6 SERVINGS.

Orange Sweet Potatoes: Substitute 3 tablespoons orange juice for the water and add 1 tablespoon grated orange peel.
Pineapple Sweet Potatoes: Omit the water and add 1 can (8¼ ounces) crushed pineapple (with syrup).
Spicy Sweet Potatoes: Stir ½ teaspoon ground cinnamon or ¼ teaspoon ground allspice, cloves, mace or nutmeg into sugar mixture in skillet.

SWEET POTATO CHIPS

Cut 4 medium pared sweet potatoes or yams (about 1 pound) into $\frac{1}{16}$-inch slices. Soak in 2 quarts ice water 1 hour. Drain and pat dry. Heat vegetable oil or shortening (3 inches) to 360° in deep fat fryer or heavy saucepan. Fry potato slices until light brown around edges, 1 to 2 minutes; drain on paper towels. Sprinkle with salt. Keep warm in oven.   4 SERVINGS.

SPINACH WITH BACON AND ONION

1 slice bacon, cut up
1 small onion, thinly sliced
1 pound spinach

¼ teaspoon salt
Dash of pepper

Cook and stir bacon and onion in 10-inch skillet until bacon is crisp. Add about half of the spinach, the salt and pepper. Cover and cook over medium heat 2 minutes. Add remaining spinach. Cover and cook, stirring occasionally, until spinach is tender, 3 to 10 minutes.   3 OR 4 SERVINGS.

The seasonal pleasure of tomatoes is still a distinct one, for despite all the modern agricultural and transportation wonders, no greenhouse has succeeded in duplicating the taste and texture of a locally grown, sun-ripened tomato.

Although native to the Western Hemisphere, the tomato came to our land by a circuitous route. It is thought that the conquistadors brought it to Europe from Mexico; but not until the late 1700s did it appear here — and then, the "love apple" was considered an aphrodisiac or, worse, poisonous. By the mid-1900s the tomato finally gained wide acceptance as a food.

In most home vegetable gardens, growers often find themselves with a sudden abundance and begin looking up recipes for Tomato Mincemeat, pickles and sauces. Fried Tomatoes and Cream Gravy is another excellent use for that summer excess.

FRIED TOMATOES AND CREAM GRAVY

½ cup cornmeal*
3 tablespoons flour
2 teaspoons sugar
2 teaspoons salt
¼ teaspoon pepper
4 firm ripe or green large
    tomatoes, cut into ¾-inch
    slices

⅓ cup butter, margarine or
    bacon fat
1 cup whipping cream
½ teaspoon salt
Snipped parsley or green onion
    tops
Crisply fried bacon, lean salt
    pork or sausage

Pictured opposite.
Your kitchen garden takes on new taste with these American classics. Clockwise from top: Wilted Lettuce Salad (page 109), Spinach with Bacon and Onion(this page), Creamed Radishes (page 104), Green Beans, Cape Cod Style (page 94) and Orange Beets (page 101).

Mix cornmeal, flour, sugar, 2 teaspoons salt and the pepper. Coat tomato slices with cornmeal mixture. Heat butter in 10-inch skillet until melted. Add tomato slices. Cook, turning once, until golden brown. Place in shallow baking dish or on platter; keep warm. Heat cream and ½ teaspoon salt to boiling in same skillet; pour over tomato slices. Sprinkle with parsley. Serve with bacon.   4 TO 6 SERVINGS.

*½ cup all-purpose flour can be substituted for the cornmeal and flour.

SALADS

Despite its name, Caesar (or California) Salad is said to have been created in Tijuana, Mexico, during the twenties. Whatever its beginnings, the original salad of romaine lettuce mixed with grated cheese, coddled eggs and bread cubes fried in olive oil started a no-end-in-sight trend. Caesar Salad quickly crossed the border and became the last word in sophisticated American restaurants. Diners managed to extricate the secret of the coddled eggs from chefs and, finally, Caesar Salad became a classic of the American home kitchen.

CAESAR SALAD

2 cloves garlic, cut in halves
4 slices white bread
⅔ cup olive oil
1 teaspoon salt
½ teaspoon pepper
2 large bunches romaine

Coddled Eggs (below)
1 lemon
½ cup grated Parmesan or
   Romano cheese
1 can (2 ounces) anchovy fillets,
   chopped

Rub large salad bowl with garlic. Trim crusts from bread; cut bread into cubes. Heat ⅓ cup of the oil in 10-inch skillet. Add garlic and bread cubes. Cook over medium heat, stirring constantly, until bread cubes are brown. Remove from heat; discard garlic.

Mix remaining ⅓ cup oil, the salt and pepper in salad bowl. Tear romaine into bite-size pieces into salad bowl. Toss until leaves glisten. Break Coddled Eggs onto romaine; squeeze juice from lemon over romaine. Toss until leaves are well coated. Add cheese, anchovies and bread cubes; toss.   8 SERVINGS.

CODDLED EGGS
Place 2 eggs in warm water. Heat enough water to completely cover eggs to boiling in saucepan. Immerse eggs in boiling water. Remove from heat; cover and let stand 30 seconds. Immediately cool eggs in cold water.

Three generations of this American family enjoy a hearty outdoor picnic.

FRESH MUSHROOM AND SPINACH SALAD

2 tablespoons tarragon or wine
   vinegar
¾ teaspoon salt
¼ teaspoon monosodium
   glutamate
1 small clove garlic, crushed

Generous dash of freshly
   ground pepper
8 ounces mushrooms, sliced
16 ounces spinach, torn into
   bite-size pieces
¼ cup vegetable oil

Mix vinegar, salt, monosodium glutamate, garlic and pepper; toss with mushrooms and let stand 15 minutes. Toss spinach and oil until leaves glisten. Toss mushroom mixture with spinach.   4 TO 6 SERVINGS.

WILTED LETTUCE SALAD

4 slices bacon, cut up
¼ cup vinegar
2 bunches leaf lettuce,
    shredded (about 4 cups)

⅓ cup chopped green onions
2 teaspoons sugar
¼ teaspoon salt
⅛ teaspoon pepper

Fry bacon until crisp in 10-inch skillet. Stir in vinegar; heat until hot. Remove skillet from heat; add lettuce and onions. Sprinkle with sugar, salt and pepper; toss 1 to 2 minutes until lettuce is wilted.   4 SERVINGS.

Dill Wilted Lettuce: Add ½ teaspoon dried dill weed and ½ teaspoon dry mustard with the vinegar.

ORANGE-AVOCADO SALAD

2 oranges, pared and sliced
2 avocados, peeled, pitted and
    cut into wedges
2 small onions, sliced and
    separated into rings

Crisp salad greens
Orange Dressing (below)

Arrange oranges, avocados and onions on salad greens on salad plates. Drizzle Orange Dressing over salads.   4 SERVINGS.

ORANGE DRESSING
¼ cup vegetable oil
1 tablespoon lemon juice
½ teaspoon grated orange peel
2 tablespoons orange juice

1 tablespoon sugar
⅛ teaspoon salt
⅛ teaspoon dry mustard

Shake all ingredients in tightly covered jar.

PICKLED EGGS ON GREENS

6 hard-cooked eggs, peeled
1 cup cider vinegar
1 cup beet liquid
⅓ cup granulated or packed
    brown sugar

½ teaspoon salt
1 small onion, chopped
4 whole cloves
Shredded greens

Place eggs in bowl or jar. Mix remaining ingredients except greens; pour over eggs. Cover and refrigerate at least 2 days. Slice eggs; serve on greens.   6 SERVINGS.

Spiced Pickled Eggs: Substitute 2 cups white vinegar for the cider vinegar and beet liquid.

The Waldorf Astoria Hotel on Park Avenue in New York was the original home of this unpretentious salad, but the walnuts were a later addition. Made with good, crisp apples and tossed together quickly, refreshing Waldorf Salad combines the three crunch textures of apples, celery and nuts. The ready availability of canned fruits and fresh fruits in season makes fruit salads year-round fare. They go well as an accompaniment to any meat.

WALDORF SALAD

2 cups diced unpared apple
1 cup diced celery
⅓ cup coarsely chopped nuts
½ cup mayonnaise or salad
  dressing

Lettuce cups
Maraschino cherries (optional)

Mix apple, celery, nuts and mayonnaise. Serve in lettuce cups and garnish with maraschino cherries.   4 TO 6 SERVINGS.

HEAVENLY HASH SALAD

1 package (6¼ ounces)
  miniature marshmallows
  (3½ cups) or 40 large
  marshmallows, quartered
1 can (20 ounces) pineapple
  chunks, drained and
  quartered (reserve syrup)

2 cups seedless green grapes
½ cup slivered blanched
  almonds
Crisp lettuce
Whipped Cream Dressing
  (below)

Mix marshmallows and reserved pineapple syrup in 3-quart bowl. Cover and refrigerate 12 to 18 hours.

Stir pineapple, grapes and almonds into marshmallow mixture. Cover and refrigerate 2 to 3 hours. Serve over lettuce with Whipped Cream Dressing.   8 TO 10 SERVINGS.

WHIPPED CREAM DRESSING

2 egg yolks, slightly beaten
2 tablespoons sugar
2 tablespoons water
2 tablespoons vinegar or lemon
  juice

¼ teaspoon dry mustard
¼ teaspoon salt
Dash of pepper
½ cup chilled whipping cream

Cook all ingredients except cream in 1-quart saucepan over medium heat, stirring constantly, until mixture thickens and boils. Boil and stir 1 minute. Remove from heat; cool. Beat cream in chilled bowl until stiff. Fold into dressing.

FRUIT SALAD WITH LIME-HONEY DRESSING

Banana
Lemon juice
Pineapple slices
Orange slices or sections

Seedless green grapes
Melon balls or slices
Crisp lettuce cups
Lime-Honey Dressing (below)

Slice banana; dip slices into lemon juice to prevent darkening. Arrange fruits in lettuce cups on salad plates. Drizzle Lime-Honey Dressing over salads.

LIME-HONEY DRESSING

¾ cup vegetable oil
½ teaspoon grated lime peel
⅓ cup fresh lime juice (about 2 limes)
⅓ cup honey

1 teaspoon dry mustard
¾ teaspoon seasoned salt
½ teaspoon paprika
⅛ teaspoon white pepper

Shake all ingredients in tightly covered jar. Refrigerate until 30 minutes before serving time. Shake before serving.

A touch of citrus does wonders for many casseroles, cakes and vegetables; it does the same for other fruits. As in the recipe above, mellow sweet fruits seem to come into their own with the piquant Lime-Honey Dressing. The same complementary sweet and sour taste is achieved in Triple-Orange Molded Salad by filling the center of a slightly tart orange ring with sweet marshmallows, coconut and pineapple. Of the hundreds of gelatin salads in American cooking, this is one of the most impressive.

TRIPLE-ORANGE MOLDED SALAD

2 cups boiling liquid (water or fruit syrup)
1 package (6 ounces) orange-flavored gelatin
1 pint orange sherbet
2 cans (11 ounces each) mandarin orange segments, drained

1 can (13¼ ounces) pineapple chunks, drained
1 cup flaked coconut
1 cup miniature marshmallows
1 cup dairy sour cream or ½ cup whipping cream, whipped

Pour boiling liquid on gelatin in bowl; stir until gelatin is dissolved. Add sherbet; stir until melted. Stir in 1 can of the orange segments (1 cup). Pour into 6-cup ring mold. Refrigerate until firm.

Mix remaining orange segments, the pineapple, coconut and marshmallows. Fold in sour cream. Refrigerate at least 3 hours. Unmold gelatin; fill center with fruit mixture.   10 TO 12 SERVINGS.

GARBANZO-KIDNEY BEAN SALAD

1 can (20 ounces) white kidney
    beans, drained
1 can (15 ounces) garbanzo
    beans, drained
1 can (15 ounces) red kidney
    beans, drained
1½ cups diced peeled tomatoes
    (about 3 medium)
1 fresh hot pepper, seeded and
    finely chopped

¾ cup chopped red or sweet
    white onion
⅔ cup chopped green or red
    pepper
⅓ cup sliced green onions
1 bottle (8 ounces) herb and
    garlic French dressing
½ teaspoon salt
2 or 3 drops red pepper sauce
Lettuce

Mix all ingredients except lettuce. Cover and refrigerate at least 3 hours, stirring occasionally. Remove bean mixture with slotted spoon to lettuce-lined salad bowl just before serving. 10 TO 12 SERVINGS.

If a picture is worth a thousand words, a taste must be worth even more—at least in the case of the avocado. Its taste has a unique quality about it that has been described as smooth, nutty and buttery. But avocado has something undefinable about it that is only avocado. Although native to Mexico, avocados were latecomers to North American cuisine and did not become popular until the thirties, when they were known as alligator pears.

Our avocados were first grown in Florida during the last century and in California at the Spanish missions, and are still grown only in those two states. The fame of the avocado, however, has spread all across the country. Many cooks are skillful with stuffed or baked avocados, chilled avocado soups and salads. Guacamole (pronounced as if the *u* were a *w*) has several uses. Great as it is as a salad, it is equally good as a cocktail dip or spread. The recipe for Orange-Avocado Salad (page 109) shows the Western and Southwestern talent for the element of surprise that characterized their cooking. A sensational contrast in taste and color.

GUACAMOLE SALAD

2 ripe avocados, peeled and
    pitted
3 tablespoons grated onion
1 tablespoon lemon or lime
    juice
1 teaspoon salt

1 canned green hot pepper,
    finely chopped
1 medium tomato, peeled,
    seeded and chopped
Shredded lettuce

Mash avocados. Add onion, lemon juice, salt and hot pepper; beat until creamy. Fold in tomato. Cover and refrigerate no longer than 3 hours. Serve on lettuce. 5 OR 6 SERVINGS.

Pictured opposite.
Zesty flavor favorites of the Southwest are combined in the colorful Garbanzo-Kidney Bean Salad. Be sure to make it ahead of time so the flavors can blend and mellow.

FRUITS

RAW APPLESAUCE

3 medium eating apples, pared and cut up	2 tablespoons lemon juice
	2 teaspoons sugar
¼ cup light corn syrup	Dash of salt

Place half of the apples and the remaining ingredients in blender container. Cover and blend 1 to 2 minutes on high speed until smooth. Add remaining apples; repeat.   ABOUT 2 CUPS APPLESAUCE.

NOTE: For variety in texture and color, use unpared apples.

Making apple butter today the old-fashioned way: in a large kettle over an open fire, with a heavy wooden paddle for stirring.

In the early years, everyone drank several mugs of cider a day—not our grocery store variety, but an alelike fermented cider with plenty of punch. This boon from the orchards was one pleasure not banned by the strict religious sects that settled America.

Johnny Appleseed, who actually existed and wandered about Ohio, Indiana and Illinois dressed in a coffee sack scattering seeds he gathered at cider mills, is not the only benefactor in the history of apple growing. Pioneers planted the orchards of Washington State with tiny plants they nurtured all the way across the country.

Of the hundreds of varieties grown, a few are marketed nationally. The Red Delicious, easily identifiable by its bumpy bottom and deep red color, is one of the best-known eating apples. It is not good for cooking. Stayman and Newtown Pippin are all-purpose apples. Golden Delicious, Winesap, Jonathan and McIntosh are excellent for eating. The tart, firm apples ideal for applesauce, apple butter and baking are Rome Beauty, York Imperial and Rhode Island Greening. Still others may be sold in your area.

Whole books on apple cookery attest to their diversity, from plain to fancy, but as with many fruits, the unadorned methods of preparation are often the most popular. Raw Applesauce and Glazed Baked Apples are two such recipes.

GLAZED BAKED APPLES

4 large baking apples	¼ teaspoon red food color
½ cup sugar	

Heat oven to 400°. Core apples; pare upper half of each apple. Place apples in ungreased baking dish, 8x8x2 inches. Pour boiling water (¼ inch deep) into baking dish. Cover with aluminum foil.

Bake 25 minutes. Sprinkle 1 tablespoon sugar over each apple. Stir food color into syrup in baking dish; spoon over apples. Bake uncovered, spooning syrup over apples occasionally, until apples are tender when pierced with fork, 20 to 25 minutes. Sprinkle 1 tablespoon sugar over each apple; spoon syrup over apples.   4 SERVINGS.

A visitor offered flummery, grunt, fool, sippit or slump for dessert probably would be inclined to refuse, which would be a pity since these odd names belong to a group of homespun desserts that are the glory of American fruit cookery.

Various crisps, pandowdies, brown Bettys, deep dish pies, cobblers and summer puddings share with them the generous use of a certain fruit gathered in season. Though battered tin berry pails no longer hang on hooks on the back porch and the word "berrying" has almost dropped from most of our vocabularies, wild berries and fruits are still abundant in the countryside. Blueberries in Maine, beach plums on Cape Cod, scuppernong grapes in North Carolina, raspberries in New Jersey and many other fruits and berries grow in tangles along out-of-the-way roadsides.

All the American fruit desserts have a delightful honesty about them, like the simple charm of a calico dress or a country garden of hollyhocks and climbing roses.

BLUEBERRY CRISP

1 package (16 ounces) frozen
    unsweetened blueberries or
    3 cups blueberries
2 tablespoons lemon juice
⅔ cup packed brown sugar
½ cup all-purpose flour

½ cup quick-cooking oats
¾ teaspoon ground cinnamon
¼ teaspoon salt
⅓ cup butter or margarine,
    softened
Cream or ice cream

Heat oven to 375°. Place blueberries in ungreased baking dish, 8x8x2 inches. Sprinkle with lemon juice. Mix remaining ingredients except cream; sprinkle over blueberries. Bake uncovered until topping is golden brown and blueberries are hot, about 30 minutes. Serve with cream.   4 to 6 SERVINGS.

CRANBERRY-ORANGE RELISH

4 cups cranberries (1 pound)
1 unpeeled orange, cut up

1½ to 2 cups sugar

Chop cranberries and orange pieces in food grinder, using fine blade. Stir in sugar. Cover and refrigerate at least 24 hours before serving. 3½ CUPS RELISH.

Cranberry-Apple Relish: Reduce cranberries to 3 cups. Chop 6 unpared medium red apples, cut up, with the cranberries and orange pieces.

NOTE: Cranberries and orange pieces can be chopped in blender following manufacturer's directions.

BROILED HONEY GRAPEFRUIT

2 grapefruit, cut in halves
¼ cup honey

8 drops aromatic bitters
(optional)

Remove seeds from grapefruit halves. Cut around edges and sections to loosen; remove centers. Mix honey and bitters; drizzle about 1 tablespoon over each grapefruit half. Set oven control to broil and/or 550°. Broil grapefruit halves with tops 5 inches from heat about 5 minutes.   4 SERVINGS.

The delicate flavor of rose water was highly prized in the nineteenth century, particularly as an accent for fruits. Although this flavoring is not common today, it is available at many drugstores and gourmet shops.

SHAKER PEACHES

3 tablespoons butter or
margarine
2 tablespoons water
6 large firm ripe peaches,
peeled, halved and pitted

Rose water
¼ cup packed brown sugar
Sweetened whipped cream or
ice cream (optional)

Heat butter in heavy 10-inch skillet until melted. Add water; place peach halves hollow sides up in skillet. Place a drop of rose water and 1 teaspoon sugar in each hollow. Cover and simmer until peaches are tender, about 20 minutes. Serve with syrup from skillet and whipped cream.   6 SERVINGS.

NOTE: Peaches can be served as a meat or poultry accompaniment.

STEWED PLUMS

2 cups water
¾ to 1 cup sugar
2 tablespoons lemon juice
⅛ teaspoon salt

Dash of ground allspice
2 cinnamon sticks
2 pounds ripe plums

Heat water, sugar, lemon juice, salt, allspice and cinnamon sticks to boiling in 3-quart saucepan. Add plums. Cook uncovered over medium heat just until plums are tender, about 15 minutes. Cool and refrigerate. Serve as a breakfast fruit, dessert or meat accompaniment.   8 SERVINGS.

NOTE: Italian prune, Santa Rosa, Greengage or Damson plums can be used in this recipe.

PRUNES IN PORT

Heat 1 pound prunes, 2 cups port or other sweet red wine and ½ cup water to boiling in 2-quart saucepan; reduce heat. Cover and simmer until tender, 10 to 15 minutes. Cool and refrigerate. Serve as a relish or dessert.

Prunes in Claret: Substitute 2 cups claret or other dry red wine for the port; stir ⅓ cup sugar into prune mixture after simmering.

NOTE: If pitted prunes are used, reduce prunes to 12 ounces. Simmer 5 minutes.

STEWED RHUBARB

¾ to 1 cup sugar
½ cup water
4 cups 1-inch pieces rhubarb

Few drops red food color
(optional)

Heat sugar and water to boiling, stirring occasionally. Add rhubarb; reduce heat. Simmer uncovered until rhubarb is tender and slightly transparent, about 10 minutes. Stir in food color.   5 SERVINGS.

FONDANT-DIPPED STRAWBERRIES

2 cups sugar
1¼ cups water
2 tablespoons light corn syrup

½ teaspoon almond extract
1 quart whole strawberries

Heat sugar, water and corn syrup to boiling in 2-quart saucepan over medium heat, stirring constantly, until sugar is dissolved. Boil, without stirring, until candy thermometer registers 240° (or until small amount of mixture dropped into very cold water forms a soft ball that flattens when removed from water). Pour onto moistened baking sheet, heatproof platter or marble slab without scraping saucepan. Cool just until lukewarm. Scrape mixture toward center of baking sheet, using broad, stiff spatula or wooden spoon. Spread mixture out again, using long, firm strokes; continue spreading until mixture is firm and white. Knead until smooth and creamy. Cover and refrigerate at least 12 hours.

Wash and thoroughly dry strawberries. Heat fondant over hot (not boiling) water until melted. Stir in almond extract and enough hot water (1 to 2 tablespoons) to make fondant dipping consistency. Dip strawberries into fondant, leaving stem ends visible. Place strawberries stem ends down on wire rack; let harden. Refrigerate no longer than 6 hours.   4 TO 5 DOZEN STRAWBERRIES.

BROILED FRESH FRUIT

Halve and pit 1 peach, nectarine or apricot or halve and core 1 pear. Make a few partial cuts through fruit. Brush each half with ¼ to ½ teaspoon butter or margarine, softened. Top halves in one of the following ways:

☐ Brush with soy sauce; sprinkle with ground ginger. Serve with pork, beef or poultry.

☐ Sprinkle with seasoned salt and pepper. Serve with lamb, veal or pork.

☐ Drizzle with lemon or lime juice; sprinkle with ½ teaspoon brown sugar and dash of ground nutmeg. Serve with smoked pork or vegetables.

☐ Drizzle with honey or maple-flavored syrup; sprinkle with ground cinnamon. Serve with ham, pork or corned beef.

☐ Spread with mixture of 2 tablespoons orange marmalade and ¼ teaspoon dry mustard. Serve with pork, beef or poultry.

☐ Drizzle with sherry or brandy; sprinkle with grated orange peel. Serve with pork, beef or poultry.

Set oven control to broil and/or 550°. Broil fruit halves with tops about 5 inches from heat until bubbly, 4 to 6 minutes.

BRANDY FRUITS

Pour 2 cups brandy into sterilized large pottery or clear glass container. Add 4 cups assorted fresh fruits* and 4 cups sugar; stir gently until sugar is dissolved. Cover tightly and let stand in cool place 3 days, then refrigerate 4 days.

Add assorted fruits (no more than 4 cups) and an equal amount of sugar at a minimum of 1-week intervals; stir gently. Cover tightly and let stand in cool place 3 days, then refrigerate at least 4 days.

Fruits can be served 1 week after the second addition of fruits and sugar or additional fruits and sugar can be added as directed above. Serve 1 week after last addition of fruits and sugar.

Serve over ice cream, sherbet, cake, custard, pudding or cut-up fruits. Or pack in jars and refrigerate indefinitely.

*Use firm ripe fruits; do not use bruised fruits. Fruits should be clean and dry. Peel, pit and cut into large slices peaches, apricots, nectarines and plums; pare, core and slice pears; remove rind, eyes and core from pineapple and cut pineapple into chunks; cut grapes in halves, removing seeds if necessary; pit cherries. Strawberries, blackberries, raspberries, currants and orange or tangerine sections can also be used. Do not use fresh apples or bananas. Unsweetened frozen fruits can be used.

Pictured opposite.
Start Brandy Fruits just as soon as fresh fruits are abundant so you can use the widest assortment possible. It makes an excellent hostess gift!

PUT-UPS

Process fruits, tomatoes and pickled vegetables in a boiling-water-bath canner. Process all common vegetables (low acid foods) in a steam-pressure canner. Wash all fruits and vegetables thoroughly whether or not they are to be pared. (Dirt contains some of the bacteria hardest to kill.)

Examine tops and edges of standard jars and lids. Discard any with cracks, chips, dents or rust. Wash jars in hot, soapy water; rinse well. Cover jars with hot water until used; invert on folded towel to drain just before filling. Prepare lids as directed by the manufacturer.

Fill water-bath canner containing a wire or wooden rack half full with hot water; heat. (Water should be hot but not boiling when jars are placed in canner.) Pack hot mixture in hot jars leaving headspace specified in each recipe. Wipe tops and screw-threads of jars with damp cloth; seal immediately as directed by manufacturer.

Place each jar, as it is filled, on rack in water bath; allow enough space for water to circulate. (Jars should not touch each other or fall against side of canner.) Add boiling water to cover jars to depth of 1 to 2 inches. (Do not pour boiling water directly on jars.) Cover canner. Heat water to boiling; reduce heat to hold water at a steady gentle boil. Start counting processing time, using time specified in each recipe. Remove jars from canner; complete seals as directed by manufacturer.

Place jars upright and several inches apart on rack or folded cloth; keep out of drafts but do not cover. Test for seal after about 12 hours (metal caps or lids will be depressed in center; lids with wire clamps and rubber seals will not leak when inverted). If seal is incomplete, empty jar, repack and reprocess food as if fresh or refrigerate for *immediate* use. Remove screw bands carefully. Store in cool, dry area.

APPLE BUTTER

4 quarts sweet apple cider	2 cups sugar
3 quarts pared and quartered cooking apples (about 4 pounds)	1 teaspoon ground cinnamon
	1 teaspoon ground ginger
	½ teaspoon ground cloves

Heat cider to boiling in 5-quart Dutch oven. Boil uncovered until cider measures 2 quarts, about 1¼ hours. Add apples. Heat to boiling; reduce heat. Simmer uncovered, stirring frequently, until apples are soft and can be broken apart with spoon, about 1 hour. (Apples can be pressed through sieve or food mill at this point if smooth apple butter is desired.)

Stir in sugar, cinnamon, ginger and cloves. Heat to boiling; reduce heat. Simmer uncovered, stirring frequently, until no liquid separates from pulp, about 2 hours. Heat to boiling. Pour into hot jars, leaving ¼-inch headspace; seal. Process 10 minutes in boiling water bath.   ABOUT 3½ PINTS.

If you've never canned, you might start with this recipe anytime at all. Apricot and Pineapple Preserves are especially easy because the fruits already are prepared. It's a particularly good choice in midwinter, when some fresh fruits might be unavailable.

APRICOT AND PINEAPPLE PRESERVES

1 package (12 ounces) dried
    apricots, cut in halves
2 cans (13¼ ounces each)
    pineapple chunks, cut
    in halves
1 jar (8 ounces) maraschino
    cherries, drained and cut
    into fourths (reserve syrup)

3 cups water
5 cups sugar
2 tablespoons lemon juice

Mix apricots, pineapple (with syrup), reserved cherry syrup and the water in 4-quart Dutch oven. Let stand 1 hour.

Stir in sugar. Heat to boiling; boil rapidly 10 minutes. Stir in lemon juice. Boil, stirring occasionally, until thickened, about 35 minutes. Stir in cherries. Pour boiling mixture into hot jars, leaving ¼-inch headspace; seal. Process 15 minutes in boiling water bath.　ABOUT 6 HALF-PINTS.

SPICED PICKLED CHERRIES

4 cans (16 ounces each) pitted
    tart water pack red cherries,
    drained, or 6 cups pitted red
    sour cherries
3 cups cider vinegar

6 cups sugar
6 whole cinnamon sticks
1 teaspoon whole allspice
1 teaspoon whole cloves

Mix cherries and vinegar in nonmetal container. Cover and refrigerate 24 hours.

Drain cherries, reserving liquid. Mix reserved cherry liquid, the sugar and spices. Heat to boiling; boil 1 minute. Pour over cherries; cool. Cover and refrigerate 24 hours.

Drain cherries, reserving syrup. Heat syrup to boiling. Pour over cherries; cool. Cover and refrigerate 24 hours. Repeat process.

Drain cherries, reserving syrup. Pack cherries in hot jars, leaving ½-inch headspace. Heat syrup to boiling. Pour over cherries, leaving ½-inch headspace; seal. Process 25 minutes in boiling water bath. Store 1 month before serving as a relish with game, poultry or meat.　4 OR 5 PINTS.

PEACH HONEY

4 pounds fully ripe medium
  peaches, peeled and coarsely
  chopped

¼ cup water
6 cups sugar

Cook peaches in water until soft. Press peaches through sieve or food mill to measure 6 cups pulp. (Or place in blender container. Cover and blend until uniform consistency.)

Mix peach pulp and sugar in 3-quart saucepan. Heat to boiling. Boil gently, stirring frequently, until mixture thickens, 20 to 25 minutes. Pour boiling mixture into hot jars, leaving ¼-inch headspace; seal. Process 10 minutes in boiling water bath.   7 OR 8 HALF-PINTS.

Spiced Peach Honey: Stir in 1 teaspoon ground cinnamon and ¼ teaspoon ground cloves with the peach pulp and sugar.

PEACH PRESERVES

4 pounds ripe peaches, peeled
  and sliced (about 8 cups)

6 cups sugar
¼ cup lemon juice

Toss peaches with sugar. Cover and refrigerate 12 to 24 hours.

Heat peach mixture to boiling, stirring constantly. Boil rapidly 20 minutes. Stir in lemon juice. Boil 10 minutes. Pour boiling mixture into hot jars, leaving ¼-inch headspace; seal. Process 15 minutes in boiling water bath.   ABOUT 6 HALF-PINTS.

Spiced Peach Preserves: Tie 8 whole cloves, 5 whole allspice, 2 cinnamon sticks, 2 blades mace and 1½ teaspoons ground coriander in cheesecloth bag; add to peach mixture before boiling. Remove spice bag before pouring mixture into jars.

Peaches have a limited growing season, so be sure to catch them while they are available, between May and October. As with other fruits for preserving, peaches should be ripe and firm—just at the peak of perfection, because, naturally, the preserve will be only as good as its ingredients. The skin color between the red areas should be yellow. The deeper and more uniform the yellow color, the riper the peach. A fully ripened peach will also yield slightly to gentle hand pressure.

A quick way to peel peaches is to dip them in boiling water for 20 to 30 seconds, then plunge them immediately into ice water. A cup of tea and a slice of warm homemade bread spread with peach preserves or peach honey is an old remedy for many small troubles.

SPICED PICKLED PEACHES

1 piece gingerroot
1 tablespoon whole allspice
1 tablespoon whole cloves
8 cups sugar

4 cups water
4 cups cider vinegar
6 pounds firm ripe small
    peaches, peeled (20 to 24)

Tie spices in cheesecloth bag. Mix spice bag, sugar, water and vinegar. Heat to boiling. Add half of the peaches. Cook just until tender, 10 to 15 minutes. Pack peaches in hot jars, leaving ¼-inch headspace. Cook remaining peaches and pack in hot jars. Remove spice bag. Heat syrup to boiling. Pour over peaches, leaving ¼-inch headspace; seal. Process 15 minutes in boiling water bath. ABOUT 5 QUARTS.

PEAR BUTTER

5 pounds pears, pared and
    sliced (about 10 cups)
¼ cup water

3 cups packed brown sugar
2 tablespoons lemon juice
½ teaspoon ground nutmeg

Cook pears in water until soft. Press through sieve or food mill to measure 6 cups pulp. (Or place in blender container. Cover and blend until uniform consistency.)

Mix pear pulp, sugar, lemon juice and nutmeg in 4-quart Dutch oven. Heat to boiling. Boil gently, stirring frequently, until mixture thickens, about 30 minutes. Pour boiling mixture into hot jars, leaving ¼-inch headspace; seal. Process 10 minutes in boiling water bath. 5 OR 6 HALF-PINTS.

PEAR CONSERVE

3 pounds winter pears, pared
    and sliced (about 8 cups)
4 cups sugar
¾ cup raisins

1 tablespoon grated orange peel
2 teaspoons grated lemon peel
¼ cup lemon juice
1 cup broken walnuts

Mix all ingredients except walnuts in 4-quart Dutch oven. Heat to boiling, stirring frequently. Boil, stirring occasionally, until mixture thickens slightly, 25 to 30 minutes. Stir in walnuts. Pour boiling mixture into hot jars, leaving ¼-inch headspace; seal. Process 15 minutes in boiling water bath. 4 OR 5 HALF-PINTS.

OLD-TIME STRAWBERRY PRESERVES

1 quart strawberries   2 tablespoons vinegar
4 cups sugar

Toss strawberries with sugar. Let stand 3 to 4 hours.

Heat strawberry mixture to boiling, stirring constantly. Boil rapidly 10 minutes. Stir in vinegar. Boil, skimming off foam, 10 minutes. Pour boiling mixture into hot jars, leaving ¼-inch headspace; seal. Process 15 minutes in boiling water bath.   ABOUT 4 HALF-PINTS.

NOTE: Be sure strawberries do not have hollow cores.

SPICED PINEAPPLE CHUNKS

2 ripe pineapples   16 whole cloves
3 cups sugar   Grated peel of 2 lemons
½ cup vinegar

Remove rind and core from pineapples; cut pineapple into chunks. Heat sugar, vinegar, cloves and lemon peel to boiling in 3-quart saucepan, stirring frequently. Add pineapple. Heat to boiling; reduce heat. Simmer uncovered, stirring occasionally, 10 minutes. Pack pineapple in hot jars, leaving ½-inch headspace. Heat syrup to boiling. Pour over pineapple, leaving ½-inch headspace; seal. Process 30 minutes in boiling water bath.   ABOUT 3 HALF-PINTS.

WATERMELON RIND PICKLES

¼ cup pickling or uniodized   1 piece gingerroot
    salt   3 sticks cinnamon, broken
8 cups cold water   2 tablespoons whole cloves
4 quarts 1-inch cubes pared   8 cups cider vinegar
    watermelon rind   9 cups sugar

Dissolve salt in cold water; pour over watermelon rind. Stir in additional water, if necessary, to cover rind. Let stand in cool place 8 hours.

Drain rind; cover with cold water. Heat to boiling. Cook just until tender, 10 to 15 minutes; drain. Tie spices in cheesecloth bag. Heat spice bag, vinegar and sugar to boiling; boil 5 minutes. Add rind; simmer 1 hour. Remove spice bag. Pack simmering mixture in hot jars, leaving ¼-inch headspace; seal. Process 10 minutes in boiling water bath.   7 OR 8 PINTS.

Pictured opposite.
"Put-by's"—a cupboard full of creative satisfaction. Some of those pictured include: Spiced Pickled Peaches (page 123), Watermelon Rind Pickles (this page), Pickled Beets and Onions (page 128) and Green Tomato Relish (page 132).

PRESERVED PUMPKIN STRIPS

1 medium pumpkin (about 7 pounds), pared
7 cups sugar

1 tablespoon plus 1 teaspoon grated lemon peel
1 cup lemon juice

Cut pumpkin into thin strips, about 2x½x⅛ inch (about 4 quarts). Place in nonmetal container. Mix with sugar. Cover and refrigerate 12 to 18 hours.

Mix pumpkin mixture, lemon peel and juice. Heat to boiling, stirring occasionally. Boil slowly until pumpkin is transparent and tender and syrup coats spoon, about 30 minutes. Pack boiling mixture in hot jars, leaving ¼-inch headspace; seal. Process 15 minutes in boiling water bath.   ABOUT 4 PINTS.

Dill has sparked the taste of pickles for hundreds of years. Among the earliest American users of dill were the Scandinavian immigrants in Wisconsin and Minnesota, who used it extensively.

Dilled Beans make a good accompaniment for picnic fried chicken. They're especially attractive when paired with bright Corn Relish or Garden Salad Pickles.

DILLED BEANS

4 quarts water
2 pounds green beans
2 cloves garlic
4 heads dill or 4 teaspoons dried dill weed
4 small dried hot peppers

2½ cups water
2 cups white vinegar
¼ cup pickling or uniodized salt

Heat 4 quarts water to boiling. Place 1 pound of the beans in wire basket; place in boiling water. Cover and boil 1 minute. Immediately plunge basket into cold water; cool 1 minute. Repeat with remaining 1 pound beans.

Pack beans vertically in hot jars, leaving ¼-inch headspace. Add ½ clove garlic, crushed, 1 head dill or 1 teaspoon dried dill weed and 1 pepper to each jar. Mix 2½ cups water, the vinegar and salt. Heat to boiling. Pour over beans, leaving ¼-inch headspace; seal. Process 10 minutes in boiling water bath. Store 2 weeks before serving. Serve chilled.   4 PINTS.

Dilled Okra: Substitute 2 pounds baby okra pods for the green beans. Blanch, pack and process as directed in recipe.

Candied Pickle Slices are put together rather than put up. Several head starts combine into a delicious, crisp pickle which tastes as though it should have been much more trouble than it is.

CANDIED PICKLE SLICES

1 quart whole sour or dill
    pickles, drained
3 cups sugar
¼ cup coarsely chopped
    pickled sweet cherry
    peppers

2 teaspoons instant minced
    onion
1 teaspoon celery seed
1 teaspoon mustard seed
½ teaspoon crushed dried hot
    peppers

Remove tips from pickles. Cut pickles into very thin slices or medium sticks; drain. Mix pickles and remaining ingredients in glass bowl. Cover and refrigerate at least 12 hours.

Stir pickle mixture until all sugar is dissolved. Pack pickles in pickle jar or several small jars. Pour syrup to rim of jar. Cover and refrigerate. Let stand at least 24 hours.   1 QUART.

NOTE: Do not use kosher-type dill pickles.

GARDEN SALAD PICKLES

3 pounds carrots, cut into strips
    1½ inches long and ⅜ inch
    wide (about 8 cups)
2 pounds wax beans, cut into
    1½-inch pieces (about 8
    cups)
8 cups water
2 teaspoons pickling or
    uniodized salt
4 medium onions, thinly sliced
    and separated into rings
    (about 4 cups)
3 medium red or green sweet
    peppers, coarsely chopped
    (about 3 cups)

3 fresh hot peppers, finely
    chopped (about 2
    tablespoons)
4 cups cider vinegar
3 cups sugar
2 tablespoons pickling or
    uniodized salt
2 tablespoons mustard seed
2 teaspoons ground turmeric
2 teaspoons paprika

Heat carrots, beans, water and 2 teaspoons salt to boiling in 8-quart Dutch oven over medium heat. Cook just until vegetables are tender, 8 to 10 minutes; drain. Stir in remaining ingredients. Heat to boiling; boil 5 minutes. Pack boiling mixture in hot jars, leaving ¼-inch headspace; seal. Process 10 minutes in boiling water bath.   8 OR 9 PINTS.

PICKLED BEETS AND ONIONS

7 pounds medium beets*
Vinegar
2½ cups sugar
2 tablespoons whole mixed
    pickling spice

2 teaspoons salt
3½ cups white vinegar
1½ cups water
2 pounds medium onions, cut
    into ¼-inch slices

Cut off all but 2 inches of beet tops; leave root ends attached. Heat enough water to cover beets to boiling. Add beets and 2 teaspoons vinegar for each quart water. Cover and heat to boiling. Cook until beets are tender, 35 to 45 minutes; drain. Run cold water over beets; slip off skins and remove root ends. Cut beets into slices.

Heat remaining ingredients to boiling in 6-quart Dutch oven; reduce heat. Simmer uncovered 10 minutes; stir in beets. Pack beets and onions in hot jars, leaving ½-inch headspace. Heat syrup to boiling. Pour over beets and onions, leaving ½-inch headspace; seal. Process 30 minutes in boiling water bath.   ABOUT 8 PINTS.

*7 cans (16 ounces each) sliced beets, drained, can be substituted for the beets.

Salt and vinegar are two basic ingredients in any pickles. Pure granulated, pickling or kosher salt are the best, if they're available. The materials that prevent caking in uniodized table salt can make the brine cloudy. The vinegar should be 40 to 60 grain with 4 to 6 percent acidity. Cider vinegar makes the flavors blend nicely but can darken light or white vegetables or fruits.

BREAD-AND-BUTTER PICKLES

3 quarts thinly sliced unpared
    cucumbers (about 4 pounds)
7 cups thinly sliced onions
    (about 2 pounds)
1 red sweet pepper, cut into
    strips
1 green pepper, cut into strips
½ cup pickling or uniodized
    salt

1 cup water
2½ cups cider or white vinegar
2½ cups sugar
2 tablespoons mustard seed
1 teaspoon celery seed
1 teaspoon ground turmeric

Mix cucumbers, onions and peppers. Dissolve salt in water; pour over vegetables. Place a solid layer of ice cubes or crushed ice over vegetables. Weight with a heavy object and let stand 3 hours.

Drain vegetables thoroughly. Mix vinegar, sugar and spices. Heat to boiling. Add vegetables; heat to boiling. Pack boiling mixture in hot jars, leaving ¼-inch headspace; seal. Process 10 minutes in boiling water bath.   ABOUT 6 PINTS.

CORN RELISH

9 ears corn
1½ cups sugar
3 tablespoons flour
2 tablespoons pickling or
    uniodized salt
2 teaspoons dry mustard
1 teaspoon ground turmeric

3 cups white vinegar
3 medium onions, chopped
2 red sweet peppers, chopped
1 green pepper, chopped
1 small head green cabbage,
    chopped

Place corn in Dutch oven; add enough cold water to cover. Heat to boiling; boil uncovered 3 minutes. Cool; cut enough kernels from corn to measure 5 cups.

Mix sugar, flour, salt, mustard and turmeric; stir in vinegar. Heat to boiling. Add vegetables. Simmer uncovered 25 minutes. Pack simmering mixture in hot jars, leaving ¼-inch headspace; seal. Process 15 minutes in boiling water bath.   5 OR 6 PINTS.

NOTE: Onions, peppers and cabbage can be ground in food grinder, using coarse blade, or chopped in blender following manufacturer's directions.

Almost everything that grows has been put-by. In early America there were delicate conserves of red roses or rosemary flowers or leaves of wood sorrel. There were walnut catsups, pickled nasturtium buds and celery vinegars. The Northeast had its spiced crab apples, and the South its pickled peaches. The Southwest put up chili relishes and the Midwest favored corn relish and tomato preserves. Out West there were olives to be brined and fruits to make into jams.

One treasure in our ancestors' china closets was a cut-glass relish dish, often divided into three or four sections that attest to the number of preserves and relishes once served at a meal. The Pennsylvania Dutch exceeded, and indeed still exceed, even that. In their tradition, every important meal includes seven sweet dishes and seven sour dishes. The sweets might include peach honey or other fruit conserve, apple butter and spiced pears. Some of the favorite sours are pickled mushrooms, dilled beans, pickled beets and spicy relishes made of cabbage, corn or peppers. The plain and frugal aspect of the main-course fare in Pennsylvania Dutch cookery becomes much less severe when considered with the fourteen surrounding "sweets" and "sours."

At county fairs there is still fierce competition for the best dill pickles and strawberry jams. Many old skills belong to the past and have faded away. But the skills of preserving, and the pleasure of seeing a shelf lined with your own preserves, are still rewarding today.

It's Fair time! And a wealth of color delights visitors to the Bloomsburg Fair in Pennsylvania.

MINCEMEAT

1½ pounds lean beef chuck
1½ pounds tart cooking apples, pared and cut into fourths (about 1 quart)
½ pound beef suet
4 ounces candied orange peel
2 ounces candied citron
1 package (15 ounces) raisins
1 package (11 ounces) currants
1½ cups packed dark brown sugar
½ teaspoon salt
1 teaspoon ground cinnamon
½ teaspoon ground cloves
½ teaspoon ground allspice
¾ cup molasses
1 cup apple cider
Grated peel of 1 lemon

Place beef chuck in 4-quart Dutch oven; add enough water to cover. Heat to boiling; reduce heat. Cover and simmer until beef is tender, about 2 hours; drain, reserving ¾ cup of the broth. Cut beef into 1-inch pieces.

Grind beef, apples, suet, orange peel, citron and raisins in food grinder, using coarse blade. Mix in 4-quart Dutch oven. Stir in currants, sugar, salt, cinnamon, cloves, allspice, molasses and reserved broth. Heat to boiling; reduce heat. Simmer uncovered, stirring just enough to prevent sticking, 1 hour. Stir in cider and lemon peel. Simmer 5 minutes. Pack simmering mixture in hot jars, leaving 1-inch headspace; seal. (Mincemeat can be frozen at this point; cool quickly, pack in freezer containers, seal and freeze. Freeze no longer than 2 months.)

Place jars on rack in steam-pressure canner containing 2 to 3 inches hot water. Fasten canner cover according to manufacturer's directions. Place canner on high heat, leaving vent open until steam escapes steadily for 10 minutes. Close vent; heat to 10 pounds pressure. Cook 25 minutes.

Remove from heat. Let pressure return to normal, 20 to 25 minutes. (Do not run water over canner to speed cooling.) Open vent and remove cover. Place jars a few inches apart out of drafts to cool.

Test for seal after 12 hours (metal caps or lids will be depressed in center; lids with wire clamps and rubber seals will not leak when inverted). If seal is incomplete, either store jars in refrigerator for immediate use or heat mincemeat to boiling, pack in hot jars and process in canner. Store jars in cool, dark place.   ABOUT 5 PINTS.

NOTE: A 6-quart pressure cooker can be used to process pint jars. Vent 1 minute; close vent and heat to 10 pounds pressure. Process 45 minutes.

Minced meats of all kinds—buffalo, venison, beef, bear—began as a way of preserving meat by pickling it. When no fresh meat was to be had, the crocks of minced meat were ready for "pyes" and meat loaves. Gradually, mincemeat became long on vegetables, fruits and spices and short on meat. The result of that switch was the relishes and dessert pies we know today.

A jar of either Green Tomato Mincemeat or traditional Mincemeat makes a very personal gift to a hostess or to a friend before a holiday when cooking can become hectic. Because of the meat in mincemeats, it is necessary to use the steam-pressure method of processing.

GREEN TOMATO MINCEMEAT

2 quarts chopped green tomatoes (about 8 pounds), drained
2 quarts chopped pared tart cooking apples (about 3 pounds)
1 cup chopped beef suet (about ¼ pound)
1 pound raisins (about 3 cups)

2⅓ cups packed dark brown sugar
1 tablespoon pickling or uniodized salt
1 tablespoon ground cinnamon
½ teaspoon ground cloves
½ teaspoon ground allspice
½ cup cider vinegar
¼ cup light molasses

Place tomatoes in 6-quart Dutch oven; add enough boiling water to cover. Heat to boiling; boil 5 minutes. Drain; return tomatoes to Dutch oven. Add enough boiling water to cover. Heat to boiling; boil 5 minutes. Drain; return tomatoes to Dutch oven.

Stir in remaining ingredients. Heat to boiling; reduce heat. Simmer uncovered, stirring frequently to prevent sticking, until thickened, ½ to 1 hour. Pack simmering mixture in hot jars, leaving 1-inch headspace; seal.

Place jars on rack in steam-pressure canner containing 2 to 3 inches hot water. Fasten canner cover according to manufacturer's directions. Place canner on high heat, leaving vent open until steam escapes steadily 10 minutes. Close vent; heat to 10 pounds pressure. Cook 25 minutes.

Remove from heat. Let pressure return to normal, 20 to 25 minutes. (Do not run water over canner to speed cooling.) Open vent and remove cover. Place jars a few inches apart out of drafts to cool.

Test for seal after 12 hours (metal caps or lids will be depressed in center; lids with wire clamps and rubber seals will not leak when inverted). If seal is incomplete, either store jars in refrigerator for immediate use or heat mincemeat to boiling, pack in hot jars and process in canner. Store jars in cool, dark place.   5 OR 6 PINTS.

NOTE: A 6-quart pressure cooker can be used to process pint jars. Vent 1 minute; close vent and heat to 10 pounds pressure. Process 45 minutes.

GREEN TOMATO RELISH

2½ cups coarsely ground red
    sweet peppers (about 6
    peppers)
2 cups coarsely ground green
    tomatoes (about 2 pounds)
2 cups coarsely ground onions
    (about 2 pounds)
2 cups coarsely ground green
    cabbage (1 small head)
1½ cups coarsely ground green
    peppers (about 3 peppers)

¼ cup pickling or uniodized
    salt
3½ cups sugar
2 cups cider vinegar
1 cup water
1 tablespoon mustard seed
1 tablespoon ground turmeric
2 teaspoons celery seed

Mix vegetables and salt. Cover and let stand 12 to 18 hours.

Drain vegetables and rinse. Mix vegetables and remaining ingredients. Heat to boiling; reduce heat. Simmer uncovered 3 minutes. Pack simmering mixture in hot jars, leaving ⅛-inch headspace; seal. Process 10 minutes in boiling water bath.   5 OR 6 PINTS.

NOTE: Vegetables can be chopped if you prefer.

SWEET PEPPER RELISH

12 large red or green sweet
    peppers, finely chopped
1 tablespoon pickling or
    uniodized salt

3 cups sugar
2 cups white vinegar

Mix peppers and salt. Cover and let stand at least 12 hours.

Drain peppers, pressing out all liquid. Heat peppers, sugar and vinegar to boiling in 3-quart saucepan, stirring frequently; reduce heat. Simmer uncovered, stirring frequently, until thickened, about 45 minutes. Pour simmering mixture into hot jars, leaving ¼-inch headspace; seal. Process 10 minutes in boiling water bath.   ABOUT 6 HALF-PINTS.

NOTE: Peppers can be ground in food grinder, using medium blade.

Pictured opposite.
An array of sweets to tempt any palate. Clockwise from top: Lemon Snow Pudding with Stirred Custard (page 148), Old-fashioned Sponge Candy (page 154), Fudge Pudding Cake (page 144), Molasses Duff with Lemon Sauce (page 143) and Popcorn Balls (page 152).

SWEETS

Americans always have had an incredible appetite and determination for sweets. One of the events that led up to the Revolutionary War was the British imposition of a tax on molasses, which was commonly used as a sweetener at that time. "I know not why we should blush to confess that molasses was an essential ingredient in American independence," John Adams wrote. Probably no one did blush; the early Americans were far too fond of their puddings and candies for that.

The oldest truly American pudding is, of course, Indian Pudding. Though made in many ways, it is basically a dish of cornmeal, which the Indians sweetened with honey or maple sugar. In their search for sweeteners, it seems that the Indians tapped into almost every stalk and tree that grew. They made a kind of candy from the juice in the cornstalk and learned to tap the sweet sap of the birch as well as the maple trees. The New England colonists quickly learned these skills and depended on them for many years. Molasses wasn't imported from the West Indies in quantity until after 1700, and refined sugar remained a luxury for the very few. Even the sight of a little cane sugar in a bowl for Sunday visitors was considered a treat.

The sweets of early America are a real lesson in how frugality and inventiveness went hand in hand. The common denominator of these desserts was the economical use of ingredients. Leftover rice, cornmeal, sweet potatoes and stale bread were transformed out of necessity into the popular and hearty puddings we still enjoy today. For ordinary meals the puddings and custards usually were served plain. For guests or holidays there were often accompanying sauces or a pitcher of "pour cream." The most desired flavoring for these puddings was nutmeg, a spice so scarce that unscrupulous peddlers frequently sold unsuspecting buyers wooden nutmegs that had been doused with nutmeg extract. Connecticut must have been particularly prey to such tactics since it is still known as the "[Wooden] Nutmeg State."

Out on the frontier, spices were rare commodities indeed; and desserts were simple. In the early days of the westward move, fruit leather was a popular use of excess fruits around orchards. Apricots, peaches and other fruits were cooked, squeezed out and put on platters to dry. When they became leathery, they were rolled into layers or strung on threads and then hung in the kitchen. Another rather primitive sweet occasionally enjoyed in wagon trains or out on the range was unappetizingly named Spotted Pup, a mixture of sweetened rice "spotted" with a handful of raisins.

In this chapter we have Spotted Pup's more elegant relative, Creamy Rice Pudding, richer with sugar and spice than its frontier cousin. Many of our pudding recipes—Hasty Pudding, Bread Pudding and Indian Pudding—would have been right at home on an early American hearth. With their original virtues of economy and pleasing taste intact, they are still delightful family desserts. Other

Collecting maple syrup in Vermont. The Indians taught the early settlers how to use maple sugar as a sweetener.

more elaborate puddings, such as Molasses Duff with Brandy-Orange Sauce, Steamed Fig Pudding and Yam Pudding, also have nostalgic connections with our heritage and are interesting choices for special occasions.

During the eighteenth century, ice cream was the most desirable and the most unobtainable sweet Americans dreamed of. It was not only rare because sugar was so expensive, but the process of making it was tricky. Until the nineteenth century, ice was hard to come by. In winter, northern settlers could chip ice from frozen streams, but in the Deep South they had to wait for a hailstorm!

Considering the difficulties of making ice cream, a surprising amount of it was served. George Washington's ice-cream bill in the summer of 1790 was equivalent to two hundred dollars, quite a sum in those days. Thomas Jefferson brought back a French cook from a trip abroad and also brought hundreds of vanilla beans to flavor his favorite vanilla ice cream, which he usually served in a pastry crust to his guests.

After ice became readily available during the nineteenth century, ice-cream parlors began to open in the cities. In 1846, the popularity of ice cream turned into a national craze when Nancy Johnson invented the hand-cranked ice-cream maker. Every family wanted one. Recipes for dozens of flavors began to appear in cookbooks. Hokey-Pokey (slang for frozen dairy treats) carts began to ply the city streets. Ice cream became almost synonymous with dessert.

Along with ice cream, candy was becoming more accessible all during the last century. When cane and beet sugar became more easily available, Americans could indulge their fancies for sweets endlessly. Without thermometers, but undaunted by vague instructions to cook to a "hard crack" or to a "fine thread," cooks began to create peanut brittle, fudge and other fancy confections such as Fondant-dipped Strawberries and Pralines in their own homes. Pulling taffy and making popcorn balls were popular at parties, and many a batch of fudge was cooked over a gaslight in women's colleges around the country. The Soldier's Fudge, Molasses Taffy, Popcorn Balls and Candy Apples on Sticks in this chapter all are good introductions to the pleasures of candy making.

Though the popularity of making candy has abated somewhat in recent years, many cooks still have a few recipes they regularly make for holidays. The candies in this section are scrumptious gifts, and most are very simple to prepare. We've chosen several that have the added advantage of requiring no cooking. Sugarplums, Bourbon Balls and Brandied Stuffed Dates can be put together in a flash. Creole Kisses are baked with ease in the oven. Only the marvelous Fresh Coconut Candy takes much effort, and it is guaranteed to be worth every minute! A selection of these candies in a jar tied with ribbon makes the most welcome gift.

These confections, puddings and special treats Americans love are as sweet as ever!

PUDDINGS

BROWN PUDDING

1 cup all-purpose flour*
1 cup packed dark brown sugar
1 teaspoon baking powder
1 teaspoon ground cinnamon
¼ teaspoon salt
½ cup milk
2 tablespoons butter or
    margarine, softened

1 cup raisins
¾ cup chopped nuts
1¾ cups water
1 cup packed light brown sugar
2 tablespoons butter or
    margarine
⅛ teaspoon salt
Cream or ice cream

Heat oven to 350°. Mix flour, dark brown sugar, baking powder, cinnamon, ¼ teaspoon salt, the milk and 2 tablespoons butter. Stir in raisins and nuts. Pour into ungreased baking pan, 9x9x2 inches. Heat water, light brown sugar, 2 tablespoons butter and ⅛ teaspoon salt, stirring frequently, until butter is melted. Pour over batter. Bake 45 minutes. Serve with cream.   9 SERVINGS.

*If using self-rising flour, omit baking powder and salt.

CORNSTARCH PUDDING

⅓ cup sugar
3 tablespoons cornstarch
¼ teaspoon salt

2¼ cups milk
1½ teaspoons vanilla

Mix sugar, cornstarch and salt in 2-quart saucepan. Stir in milk gradually. Cook over medium heat, stirring constantly, until mixture thickens and boils. Boil and stir 1 minute. Remove from heat; stir in vanilla. Pour into dessert dishes. Cool slightly; refrigerate.   4 SERVINGS.

CREAMY RICE PUDDING

1 cup water
½ cup uncooked regular rice
½ teaspoon salt
2½ cups milk

¼ cup sugar
¼ teaspoon ground cinnamon
    or nutmeg
½ cup raisins (optional)

Heat oven to 350°. Heat water, rice and salt to boiling in 2-quart saucepan; reduce heat. Cover and simmer 10 minutes. Stir remaining ingredients into rice. Pour into ungreased 1½-quart casserole. Place casserole in pan of very hot water (1 inch deep).

Bake, stirring occasionally, until most of the milk is absorbed, 1½ to 1¾ hours.   6 TO 8 SERVINGS.

When oven temperatures were determined by the cook putting her fist in the oven and counting out "One potato, two potato . . ." or by tossing in a spoonful of flour and counting the seconds until it browned, it was only natural that the country's first desserts would not be too fussy. Often they were simply steamed over the fire, even outdoors if the family happened to be traveling.

America's heritage puddings, made with the most basic ingredients, illustrate the bird-in-hand necessity that launched American cooking. Their essence, too, embodies another early virtue—hospitality. There always was room for one more at the long harvest tables set with pewter tankards of cider and steaming bowls of Indian Pudding.

Today, many of these puddings seem especially appropriate for holiday meals. Or offer one as the final course at a friendly potluck party with each guest bringing an early American dish.

HASTY PUDDING

¾ cup cornmeal
¾ cup cold water
2½ cups boiling water
¾ teaspoon salt

Butter, margarine or light
  cream
Molasses or sugar

Mix cornmeal and cold water in 2-quart saucepan. Stir in boiling water and salt. Cook over medium heat, stirring constantly, until mixture thickens and boils; reduce heat. Cover and cook over low heat 10 minutes. Serve hot with butter and molasses as a cereal or dessert.   4 SERVINGS.

INDIAN PUDDING

½ cup cornmeal
4 cups milk, scalded
¼ cup molasses
3 eggs, well beaten

¼ cup sugar
¾ teaspoon salt
½ teaspoon ground ginger
Cream (optional)

Heat oven to 350°. Stir cornmeal into milk. Cook over low heat, stirring occasionally, until mixture coats metal spoon, about 10 minutes. Stir in molasses. Mix eggs, sugar, salt and ginger. Stir in hot cornmeal mixture gradually. Pour into ungreased 1½-quart casserole. Place casserole in pan of very hot water (1 inch deep).

Bake until knife inserted halfway between edge and center of pudding comes out clean and pudding is golden, about 1 hour. Serve hot with cream.   6 SERVINGS.

STEAMED FIG PUDDING

1 cup boiling water	1 teaspoon baking soda
1 cup finely cut-up dried figs	1 teaspoon salt
2 tablespoons shortening	1 cup chopped nuts
1½ cups all-purpose flour*	1 egg
1 cup sugar	Creamy Sauce (below)

Pour boiling water over figs; stir in shortening. Mix flour, sugar, baking soda, salt and nuts in 2-quart bowl. Stir in fig mixture and egg. Pour into well-greased 6-cup mold. Cover with aluminum foil.

Place mold on rack in Dutch oven or steamer; pour boiling water into pan halfway up mold. Cover pan. Keep water boiling over low heat until wooden pick inserted in center of pudding comes out clean, about 1½ hours.

Remove mold from pan and let stand 5 minutes; unmold. Serve warm with Creamy Sauce.   8 SERVINGS.

*Do not use self-rising flour in this recipe.

CREAMY SAUCE
Beat ¾ cup powdered sugar and ¾ cup butter or margarine, softened, in 1-quart saucepan until smooth and creamy. Stir in ¾ cup whipping cream. Heat to boiling, stirring occasionally. Serve immediately.

YAM PUDDING

3½ cups grated uncooked yams or sweet potatoes (about 2 pounds)	½ cup packed brown sugar
	1 teaspoon ground cinnamon
1¼ cups milk	½ teaspoon salt
½ cup light corn syrup	½ teaspoon ground nutmeg
3 eggs, beaten	Cream or ice cream
2 tablespoons butter or margarine, softened	

Heat oven to 325°. Mix all ingredients except cream. Pour into greased baking dish, 8x8x2 inches.

Bake until knife inserted halfway between edge and center of pudding comes out clean, about 1 hour. Serve with cream.   6 TO 8 SERVINGS.

NOTE: To grate yams easily, use a blender following manufacturer's directions.

Pictured opposite.
Puddings hold a justifiably secure position in our culinary heritage. Left: Creamy Rice Pudding (page 136). Right: Date and Nut Pudding (page 140). Bottom: Steamed Fig Pudding with Creamy Sauce (this page).

DATE AND NUT PUDDING

3 eggs
¾ cup sugar
¾ cup all-purpose flour*
1½ teaspoons baking powder
½ teaspoon salt
1½ cups cut-up dates
¾ cup coarsely chopped nuts
Partially whipped cream

Heat oven to 325°. Beat eggs in small mixer bowl until light and fluffy, about 3 minutes. Beat in sugar gradually; continue beating until very thick. Stir in flour, baking powder and salt. Stir in dates and nuts. Pour into greased 9-inch pie plate or baking pan, 9x9x2 inches.

Bake until wooden pick inserted near center of pudding comes out clean, 45 to 55 minutes. Serve warm with whipped cream.   8 OR 9 SERVINGS.

*If using self-rising flour, omit baking powder and salt.

Prunes, dates, yams, figs and apples all make notable puddings, each somewhat regional in character. The origin of Ozark Pudding is obvious from its name, but it is a close kin to many puddings that are baked wherever there are apple orchards. Yam Pudding is Southern, but sweets made from carrots, pumpkins and other vegetables are characteristic of different areas. The dried fruit puddings—date, fig and prune—are only representative of the imaginative use of reconstituted fruits in our cookery. In most of these puddings the plentiful use of nuts indicates the abundance of wild nut trees in many areas of early America.

OZARK PUDDING

¾ cup sugar
⅓ cup all-purpose flour*
1½ teaspoons baking powder
⅛ teaspoon salt
1 egg
1 teaspoon vanilla
1 medium apple, pared and
    finely chopped (about 1 cup)
½ cup chopped nuts
Sweetened whipped cream, ice
    cream or hard sauce

Heat oven to 350°. Beat sugar, flour, baking powder, salt, egg and vanilla in small mixer bowl on medium speed until smooth, about 1 minute. Stir in apple and nuts. Pour into greased 8- or 9-inch pie plate.

Bake until golden brown, about 30 minutes. Cut into wedges. Serve warm with whipped cream.   6 SERVINGS.

*If using self-rising flour, reduce baking powder to 1 teaspoon and omit salt.

As much a part of the first kitchens as the iron skillet or the long white apron, bread pudding in its many artless guises endures as a useful and infinitely variable sweet. Perfectly plain, it is an appealing dessert after a spicy meal, but there are so many embellishments that the recipe below may be considered only a starting point for you. In the past, cooks served bread puddings with a berry puree, a lemon sauce or a sauce made from dried fruits. Sometimes the pudding was baked with layers of fruit or preserves, or perhaps with a handful of coconut or nuts.

Everyone, from adamant meat-and-potatoes fans to jaded gourmets, responds to the innocence of a well-made bread pudding.

OLD-FASHIONED BREAD PUDDING

2 cups milk
¼ cup butter or margarine
3 cups soft bread crumbs (3 to 4 slices bread)
½ cup sugar
1 teaspoon ground cinnamon or nutmeg
¼ teaspoon salt
2 eggs, slightly beaten
½ cup raisins (optional)

Heat oven to 350°. Heat milk and butter over medium heat until butter is melted and milk is scalded. Mix remaining ingredients in ungreased 1½-quart casserole; stir in milk mixture. Place casserole in pan of very hot water (1 inch deep).

Bake until knife inserted 1 inch from edge of pudding comes out clean, 40 to 45 minutes. Serve warm.   6 TO 8 SERVINGS.

OLD-FASHIONED TAPIOCA PUDDING

6 cups water
¾ cup pearl tapioca
2 cups milk
2 eggs, separated
½ cup sugar
¼ teaspoon salt
1 teaspoon vanilla

Pour water over tapioca; let stand about 12 hours.

Drain tapioca. Mix tapioca and milk in top of double boiler. Cover and cook over hot water, stirring occasionally, until tapioca is transparent, about 1 hour.

Beat egg yolks, ¼ cup of the sugar and the salt. Stir about half of the tapioca mixture gradually into egg yolk mixture; stir into hot tapioca mixture in pan. Cook over hot water, stirring frequently, 5 minutes. Remove from heat; stir in vanilla. Cool slightly. Beat egg whites until foamy. Beat in remaining ¼ cup sugar, 1 tablespoon at a time; continue beating until stiff and glossy. Fold tapioca mixture into egg whites.   8 TO 10 SERVINGS.

BAKED PRUNE WHIP

1 cup pitted prunes, cooked and
   cut up
⅓ cup sugar
¼ teaspoon salt

3 egg whites
1 tablespoon lemon juice
¼ cup chopped pecans
Sweetened whipped cream

Heat oven to 350°. Beat prunes, sugar, salt and egg whites in small mixer bowl until stiff. Fold in lemon juice and pecans. Spread in ungreased 1½-quart casserole. Place casserole in pan of very hot water (1 inch deep).

Bake until pudding is puffed and a thin film has formed on top, 30 to 35 minutes. Serve warm with whipped cream.   4 TO 6 SERVINGS.

Dumplings of all kinds were at one time a far more important part of the regular fare. Plain or mincemeat dumplings were economical and could be cooked quickly on the trail with whatever flour or grain was available. In dessert cookery, fruits often were cooked in the dumplings. These are unusual in that they are plain dumplings served for dessert.

DUMPLINGS IN CARAMEL SAUCE

Caramel Sauce (below)
1½ cups all-purpose flour* or
   1⅔ cups cake flour
½ cup sugar
1½ teaspoons baking powder
½ teaspoon salt

½ cup milk
1 tablespoon butter or
   margarine, melted
Cream or sweetened whipped
   cream

Prepare Caramel Sauce. Mix remaining ingredients except cream just until flour is moistened. Drop dough by 8 spoonfuls into boiling sauce. Cover and cook over low heat until dumplings are fluffy, about 15 minutes. Serve with cream.   8 SERVINGS.

*If using self-rising flour, omit baking powder and salt.

CARAMEL SAUCE

1½ cups sugar
2 cups boiling water
1½ teaspoons vanilla

2 tablespoons butter or
   margarine

Heat sugar in heavy 10-inch skillet, stirring constantly, until sugar is melted and golden. Remove from heat; stir in boiling water slowly. Cook over low heat, stirring constantly, until sugar lumps are dissolved. Stir in vanilla and butter. Heat to boiling; boil 2 minutes.

Sauces traditionally enhanced steamed puddings on festive occasions—and often they were laced with a bit of brandy. The pudding molds themselves were often as treasured as the pudding recipes.

MOLASSES DUFF

1 egg
½ cup molasses
2 tablespoons sugar
2 tablespoons shortening
½ cup boiling water

1⅓ cups all-purpose flour*
1 teaspoon baking soda
¼ teaspoon salt
Brandy-Orange Sauce
    or Lemon Sauce (below)

Beat egg in small mixer bowl until thick. Beat in molasses and sugar on low speed. Melt shortening in boiling water; stir into molasses mixture. Beat in flour, baking soda and salt on low speed. Pour into well-greased 4-cup mold. Cover with aluminum foil.

Place mold on rack in Dutch oven or steamer; pour boiling water into pan halfway up mold. Cover pan. Keep water boiling over low heat until wooden pick inserted in center of pudding comes out clean, about 1½ hours.

Remove mold from pan and let stand 5 minutes; unmold. Serve warm with Brandy-Orange Sauce.   6 SERVINGS.

*Do not use self-rising flour in this recipe.

BRANDY-ORANGE SAUCE
3 tablespoons powdered sugar
2 egg yolks
1 teaspoon grated orange peel

2 tablespoons orange juice
1 to 2 tablespoons brandy
½ cup chilled whipping cream

Beat sugar, egg yolks and orange peel in small mixer bowl until thick. Beat in orange juice and brandy on low speed. Beat whipping cream in chilled bowl until stiff; fold in orange mixture. Serve immediately or refrigerate up to 1 hour.

LEMON SAUCE
½ cup sugar
2 tablespoons cornstarch
¼ teaspoon salt
1 cup water

2 tablespoons butter or
    margarine
1 teaspoon grated lemon peel
2 tablespoons lemon juice

Mix sugar, cornstarch and salt in 1-quart saucepan. Stir in water gradually. Cook over medium heat, stirring constantly, until mixture thickens and boils. Boil and stir 1 minute. Remove from heat; stir in butter, lemon peel and juice. Serve warm.

NOTE: Sauce can be made ahead of time. Reheat over low heat, stirring constantly.

FUDGE PUDDING CAKE

1 cup all-purpose flour*
¾ cup granulated sugar
2 tablespoons cocoa
2 teaspoons baking powder
¼ teaspoon salt
½ cup milk
2 tablespoons vegetable oil

1 teaspoon vanilla
1 cup chopped nuts (optional)
1 cup packed brown sugar
¼ cup cocoa
1¾ cups hottest tap water
Ice cream

Heat oven to 350°. Mix flour, granulated sugar, 2 tablespoons cocoa, the baking powder and salt in ungreased baking pan, 9x9x2 inches. Stir in milk, oil and vanilla with fork until smooth. Stir in nuts. Spread evenly in pan. Sprinkle with brown sugar and ¼ cup cocoa. Pour *hot* water over batter.

Bake 40 minutes. Let stand 15 minutes. Spoon into dessert dishes or cut into squares and invert on dessert plates. Top with ice cream and spoon sauce over each serving.   9 SERVINGS.

*If using self-rising flour, omit baking powder and salt.

BAKED CUSTARD

3 eggs, slightly beaten
⅓ cup sugar
Dash of salt

1 teaspoon vanilla
2½ cups milk, scalded
Ground nutmeg

Heat oven to 350°. Mix eggs, sugar, salt and vanilla. Stir in milk gradually. Pour into 6 ungreased 6-ounce custard cups. Sprinkle with nutmeg. Place cups in baking pan, 13x9x2 inches; pour very hot water into pan to within ½ inch of tops of cups. Bake until knife inserted halfway between edge and center of custard comes out clean, about 45 minutes. Remove cups from pan; cool. Serve warm or cold.   6 SERVINGS.

Baked Caramel Custard: Heat ½ cup sugar in small heavy pan over low heat, stirring constantly, until sugar melts and becomes a golden brown syrup. Divide syrup among custard cups; tilt each cup so that syrup coats bottom. Allow syrup to harden in cups, about 10 minutes. Prepare custard; pour into cups. Bake as directed. Remove cups from pan; unmold. Serve warm or cold.

When Prohibitionists succeeded in outlawing the demon rum, the popularity of ice cream soared. The soda fountain became a social center in every town, and the soda jerk a local hero who concocted enormous banana splits, sundaes and sodas. When the zealous days of

Prohibition ended, manufacturers feared ice-cream sales would decline, but they need not have worried. Ice cream is more in demand than ever!

To make these ice creams you'll need an electric or hand-crank ice-cream freezer. If you use an electric freezer, be sure to follow the manufacturer's directions carefully.

PHILADELPHIA ICE CREAM

1 quart whipping cream   2 tablespoons vanilla
¾ cup sugar   ⅛ teaspoon salt

Mix all ingredients. Pour into freezer can; put dasher in place. Cover can and adjust crank. Place can in freezer tub. Fill freezer tub ⅓ full of ice; add remaining ice alternately with layers of rock salt (6 parts ice to 1 part rock salt). Turn crank until it turns with difficulty. Draw off water. Remove lid; take out dasher. Pack mixture down; replace lid. Repack in ice and rock salt. Let ripen several hours.   1½ QUARTS ICE CREAM.

STRAWBERRY ICE CREAM

1 pint strawberries   2 cups whipping cream
1 cup sugar   1 teaspoon vanilla
¼ teaspoon salt   Few drops red food color
1 cup milk   (optional)
3 egg yolks, beaten

Mash strawberries with ½ cup of the sugar; reserve. Mix remaining ½ cup sugar, the salt, milk and egg yolks in 3-quart saucepan. Cook over medium heat, stirring constantly, just until bubbles appear around edge. Cool to room temperature. Stir in cream, vanilla, strawberries and food color.

Pour into freezer can; put dasher in place. Cover can and adjust crank. Place can in freezer tub. Fill freezer tub ⅓ full of ice; add remaining ice alternately with layers of rock salt (6 parts ice to 1 part rock salt). Turn crank until it turns with difficulty. Draw off water. Remove lid; take out dasher. Pack mixture down; replace lid. Repack in ice and rock salt. Let ripen several hours.   ABOUT 1 QUART ICE CREAM.

Peach Ice Cream: Substitute 4 or 5 peeled ripe peaches for the strawberries (mashed peaches should measure 2 cups). Stir ½ cup of the sugar into peaches.

The old-time ice-cream parlor has delighted (and dismayed!) ice-cream lovers for decades.

Going to Lindy's for cheesecake used to be as much a part of a visit to New York as seeing the Statue of Liberty. New Yorkers, too, stopped in at Lindy's after the theater or a day of shopping. Even before Lindy's closed, its famous recipe became the standard by which all other cheesecakes were measured.

Originally, the German immigrants' *käse kuchen* had a zwieback crust, and some still prefer that to pastry. Cheesecake always has been popular as a Jewish dessert after dairy meals.

The large number of servings in a rich cheesecake makes it a perfect choice when you're feeding a crowd. Sliced peaches or strawberries often are served on top with the whipped cream, but purists would say this is gilding the lily.

LINDY'S CHEESECAKE

1 cup all-purpose flour	¼ teaspoon salt
¼ cup sugar	1 tablespoon grated orange peel
½ cup butter or margarine, softened	1 tablespoon grated lemon peel
1 egg yolk	5 eggs
1 tablespoon grated lemon peel	2 egg yolks
5 packages (8 ounces each) cream cheese, softened	¼ cup whipping cream
1¾ cups sugar	¾ cup chilled whipping cream
3 tablespoons flour	⅓ cup toasted slivered almonds (optional)

Heat oven to 400°. Grease 9-inch springform pan lightly; remove bottom. Mix 1 cup flour, ¼ cup sugar, the butter, 1 egg yolk and 1 tablespoon lemon peel with hands. Press ⅓ of the mixture evenly on bottom of pan; place on baking sheet.

Bake until golden, 8 to 10 minutes; cool. Assemble bottom and side of pan; secure side. Press remaining mixture all the way up side of pan.

Heat oven to 475°. Beat cream cheese, 1¾ cups sugar, 3 tablespoons flour, the salt, orange peel, 1 tablespoon lemon peel and 2 of the eggs in large mixer bowl until smooth. Continue beating, adding remaining eggs and 2 egg yolks, 1 at a time. Beat in ¼ cup whipping cream on low speed. Pour into pan.

Bake 15 minutes. Reduce oven temperature to 200°. Bake 1 hour. Turn off oven; leave cheesecake in oven 15 minutes. Cool ½ hour. Refrigerate at least 12 hours.

Loosen cheesecake from side of pan; remove side, leaving cake on bottom of pan. Beat ¾ cup whipping cream in chilled bowl until stiff. Spread whipped cream over top of cheesecake and decorate with almonds.   20 TO 22 SERVINGS.

Pictured opposite.
Lindy's Cheesecake is not only distinguished by its origin but also by its unique pastry crust. It's delicious!

MAPLE FRANGO

4 egg yolks
½ cup maple-flavored syrup

1 cup chilled whipping cream
½ teaspoon vanilla

Beat egg yolks in small mixer bowl until thick and lemon colored, about 5 minutes. Heat syrup just to boiling. Pour about half of the hot syrup very slowly in thin stream into egg yolks, beating constantly on medium speed. Stir egg yolk mixture into hot syrup in saucepan. Cook over low heat, stirring constantly, until slightly thickened; cool.

Beat whipping cream in chilled bowl until stiff. Fold in vanilla and egg yolk mixture. Pour into ice cube tray. Freeze until firm, at least 4 hours.   6 SERVINGS.

LEMON SNOW PUDDING

1 cup sugar
1 envelope unflavored gelatin
1¼ cups water
1 teaspoon grated lemon peel

¼ cup lemon juice
3 egg whites
Dash of salt
Stirred Custard (below)

Mix sugar and gelatin in 3-quart saucepan; stir in water. Cook over medium heat, stirring constantly, just until mixture boils. Remove from heat; stir in lemon peel and juice. Chill in bowl of ice and water or refrigerate until mixture mounds slightly when dropped from spoon.

Beat egg whites and salt in small mixer bowl until soft peaks form. Beat gradually into gelatin mixture in saucepan; continue beating on high speed until mixture begins to hold its shape, about 4 minutes.

Pour into ungreased 5-cup mold or into 6 to 8 individual molds. Refrigerate until set, at least 2 hours. Unmold and serve with Stirred Custard.   6 TO 8 SERVINGS.

STIRRED CUSTARD
3 tablespoons sugar
Dash of salt
2 eggs, slightly beaten

1⅔ cups milk
½ teaspoon vanilla

Mix sugar, salt and eggs in top of double boiler. Stir in milk gradually. Place over simmering water (water should not touch bottom of pan). Cook, stirring constantly, until mixture coats metal spoon, about 20 minutes. Remove pan from simmering water; stir in vanilla. Place top of double boiler in bowl of cold water until custard is cool; refrigerate.

Until the advent of the home candy thermometer, after World War I, candy making was often a matter of know-how and good timing. But that didn't stop adventuresome American cooks from developing regional candy favorites—including some that need no cooking.

CANDIES

BOURBON BALLS

2 cups finely crushed vanilla
    wafers (about 50)
2 cups finely chopped pecans or
    walnuts (about 8 ounces)
2 cups powdered sugar

¼ cup cocoa
½ cup bourbon
¼ cup light corn syrup
Granulated sugar or chocolate
    shot

Mix crushed wafers, pecans, powdered sugar and cocoa. Stir in bourbon and corn syrup. Shape mixture into 1-inch balls. Roll in granulated sugar. Refrigerate in tightly covered container several days before serving.   ABOUT 5 DOZEN CANDIES.

Brandy Balls: Substitute ½ cup brandy for the bourbon.

Rum Balls: Substitute ½ cup light rum for the bourbon.

Because 60 to 65 percent of a date is natural sugar, it is known as the candy that grows on trees. And the brandy and pecans in this confection enhance the date's naturally sweet talents.

Date trees were first brought to the Western world by Spanish missionaries. Virtually all the dates that are sold in America come from the arid valley around Indio, California. There, a vast oasis of palms springs up from the desert, and unwary travelers arriving there might imagine they've come upon the set for an exotic movie. Actually, Indio is a lively town that revolves around the cultivation of this unique fruit. After the harvest each February, a festival is held and a Queen Scheherazade is crowned. In literature, Scheherazade told tales for 1001 nights, but Indio's Scheherazade could probably recite 1001 uses for the versatile date.

BRANDIED STUFFED DATES

1 pound pitted dates
1 cup brandy

1 cup pecan halves
Sugar (optional)

Soak dates in brandy, turning occasionally, until most of the brandy is absorbed, about 24 hours. Stuff a pecan half in each date; press to close. Roll in sugar. Refrigerate in tightly covered container.   ABOUT 1 POUND CANDIES.

Cotton candy, Candy Apples on Sticks (page 152) and Corn Dogs (page 90) are part of the fun at a fair—or anywhere.

FRESH COCONUT CANDY

1 coconut
2 cups sugar
¼ cup light corn syrup

½ teaspoon vanilla
10 to 12 candied cherries, cut in
  halves (optional)

Heat oven to 350°. Pierce eyes at 1 end of coconut with ice pick or screwdriver; drain liquid. Add enough water, if necessary, to measure ¾ cup liquid; refrigerate. Place coconut in shallow pan.

Bake until coconut cracks in several places, about 30 minutes. Reduce oven temperature to 250°. Remove coconut shell (tapping lightly, if necessary, with a hammer to break open) and pare brown skin. Grate enough coconut to measure 1 cup, packed. (Use grater or blender; do not shred.) Spread grated coconut on baking sheet. Dry in oven 15 minutes; cool.

Heat sugar, corn syrup and coconut liquid to boiling in 2-quart saucepan over medium heat, stirring constantly, until sugar is dissolved. Boil, without stirring, until candy thermometer registers 240° (or until small amount of mixture dropped into very cold water forms a soft ball that flattens when removed from water).

Pour onto moistened baking sheet, heatproof platter or marble slab without scraping saucepan. Cool just until lukewarm. Scrape mixture toward center of baking sheet, using broad, stiff spatula or wooden spoon. Spread mixture out again with spatula, using long, firm strokes; continue spreading until mixture is firm and white. Knead until smooth and creamy, working vanilla and grated coconut into mixture.

Heat mixture over hot (not boiling) water until melted. Drop by teaspoonfuls onto waxed paper. Top each candy with cherry half. Let stand until dry. Wrap individually in plastic wrap or waxed paper.   20 TO 24 CANDIES.

CREOLE KISSES

2 egg whites
¾ cup sugar

1 teaspoon vanilla
¾ cup finely chopped pecans

Heat oven to 300°. Beat egg whites in small mixer bowl until foamy. Beat in sugar, 1 tablespoon at a time; continue beating until very stiff and glossy. Stir in vanilla and pecans. Drop mixture by rounded teaspoonfuls 2 inches apart onto greased baking sheet.

Bake until dry, about 20 minutes (do not let candies brown). Immediately remove from baking sheet.   ABOUT 2 DOZEN CANDIES.

Pictured opposite.
Candy has always played an important role in satisfying America's sweet tooth. From top: Fresh Coconut Candy and Creole Kisses (both this page), Candied Orange Peel (page 156), Bourbon Balls (page 149) and Soldier's Fudge (page 155).

Candy apples go with the memory of circus music and the first glimpse of the sword swallower. Those huge trays of brightly enameled apples are still irresistible to anyone under twelve. Making them at home for a Halloween or birthday party is fun even for the adults who assist.

Decorating a Christmas tree with gingerbread men, strings of cranberries and popcorn goes along naturally with making popcorn balls. Any of the balls not devoured on the spot can be wrapped and also hung as ornaments.

Though we tend to associate popcorn balls with Christmas, popcorn originally was eaten at Thanksgiving. At the first Thanksgiving feast, Chief Massasoit's brother went into the woods and came back with bowls of popped corn, which the Pilgrims had never seen before. It's been a popular American snack food ever since.

CANDY APPLES ON STICKS

8 to 10 medium red apples	1 teaspoon red food color
2 cups sugar	Few drops oil of cloves
¾ cup water	(optional)
½ cup light corn syrup	

Insert wooden skewer in blossom end of each apple. Mix sugar, water, corn syrup and food color in top of double boiler. Heat to boiling. Boil over direct heat, without stirring, until candy thermometer registers 280° (or until a few drops of syrup dropped into very cold water separate into threads that are hard but not brittle). Stir in oil of cloves. Immediately place over boiling water in bottom of double boiler. Dip apples quickly in syrup, twirling until completely coated. Place on well-greased baking sheet; cool.   8 TO 10 CANDY APPLES.

POPCORN BALLS

½ cup sugar	Few drops food color
½ cup light corn syrup	8 cups popped corn (about ½
¼ cup butter or margarine	cup unpopped)
½ teaspoon salt	Butter or margarine

Heat sugar, corn syrup, ¼ cup butter, the salt and food color to simmering in 4-quart Dutch oven over medium-high heat, stirring constantly. Add popped corn. Cook and stir until corn is well coated, about 3 minutes. Cool slightly.

Shape mixture into 2-inch balls with hands dipped in cold water. Place on waxed paper; cool. Wrap individually in plastic wrap or place in plastic bags and tie.   1 DOZEN POPCORN BALLS.

MOLASSES NUT BRITTLE

1 cup dark corn syrup
½ cup sugar
½ cup light molasses

¼ cup butter or margarine
2 cups salted peanuts
¼ teaspoon baking soda

Butter jelly roll pan, 15½x10½x1 inch. Heat corn syrup, sugar, molasses and butter to boiling in 2-quart saucepan, stirring constantly. Stir in peanuts; heat to boiling. Boil, stirring frequently, until candy thermometer registers 280° (or until small amount of mixture dropped into very cold water separates into threads that are hard but not brittle). Watch carefully so mixture does not burn. Immediately remove from heat; stir in baking soda. Pour into pan and quickly spread evenly. Cool; break candy into pieces. ABOUT 1 POUND CANDY.

Great-grandmother's memories of taffy pulls were as treasured as her old dance cards and the thin flowers pressed in the family Bible. Perhaps she met her favorite beau while pulling the long strands of taffy at her best friend's house. Moreover, if taffy pulls were as common as the literature indicates, she probably consumed far too much candy over the course of her adolescence. Today, for a Scout troop or a slumber party, taffy pulls are a novel entertainment, and the candy is as delicious as ever.

Molasses Taffy is the long-standing American favorite, but others have their advocates. Butterscotch was a late nineteenth-century fancy, and the saltwater taffy sold along the boardwalk in Atlantic City, New Jersey, is still shipped home by visitors from all over the world. With each piece wrapped in a twist of pastel waxed paper, that easily recognizable candy has become a hallmark of its native city.

MOLASSES TAFFY

1½ cups sugar
1½ cups light molasses
½ cup water

3 tablespoons butter or
    margarine
1 tablespoon vinegar

Butter baking pan, 13x9x2 inches. Heat all ingredients to boiling in 3-quart saucepan over medium heat, stirring constantly. Boil, stirring constantly, until candy thermometer registers 256° (or until small amount of mixture dropped into very cold water forms a hard ball). Pour into pan; cool.

When just cool enough to handle, pull taffy until satiny, light in color and stiff. Butter hands lightly if taffy becomes sticky. Pull into long strips ½ inch wide. Cut with scissors into 1-inch pieces. ABOUT 1½ POUNDS CANDY.

OLD-FASHIONED SPONGE CANDY

1 cup sugar
1 cup dark corn syrup

1 tablespoon cider vinegar
1 tablespoon baking soda

Heat sugar, corn syrup and vinegar to boiling in 2-quart saucepan over medium heat, stirring constantly, until sugar is dissolved. Boil, without stirring, until candy thermometer registers 300° (or until small amount of mixture dropped into very cold water separates into threads that are hard and brittle). Remove from heat; stir in baking soda quickly and thoroughly. Pour mixture into ungreased baking pan, 13x9x2 inches. Do not spread. Cool; break candy into pieces. Serve as candy or crush and sprinkle over ice cream, pudding or fruit.   1 POUND CANDY (5 CUPS CRUSHED).

The origin of pralines is traced to a French diplomat named Plessis-Praslin, whose butler prepared special sugar-coated almonds to cure his master's indigestion. Whether they succeeded or not isn't known, but his recipe came to America with the French settlers in New Orleans. Using the native pecans and brown sugar, the Creoles' adaptation of that cure became their most famous confection, perhaps the sweetest of all sweets.

PRALINES

2 cups packed light brown
   sugar
1 cup granulated sugar
1¼ cups milk
¼ cup light corn syrup

⅛ teaspoon salt
1 teaspoon vanilla
1½ cups pecan halves (5½
   ounces)

Heat brown sugar, granulated sugar, milk, corn syrup and salt to boiling in 3-quart saucepan, stirring constantly. Boil, without stirring, until candy thermometer registers 236° (or until small amount of mixture dropped into very cold water forms a soft ball that flattens when removed from water). Immediately remove thermometer. Cool, without stirring, until saucepan is cool to the touch, about 1½ hours.

Add vanilla and pecans. Beat with spoon until mixture is slightly thickened and just coats pecans but does not lose its gloss, about 1 minute. Drop by spoonfuls onto waxed paper. (Try to divide pecans equally.) Cool until candies are firm and no longer glossy, 12 to 18 hours.

Wrap individually in plastic wrap or waxed paper and store in tightly covered container.   ABOUT 1½ DOZEN CANDIES.

Fudge and penuche are luscious tempters, fun to make and fun to eat. Both keep well if stored between layers of waxed paper in an airtight container. Over the years tons of these candies have traveled through the U.S. mails to homesick campers, students and servicemen and women.

SOLDIER'S FUDGE

1 can (14 ounces) sweetened
    condensed milk
1 package (12 ounces)
    semisweet chocolate chips
1 square (1 ounce) unsweetened
    chocolate (optional)

1 teaspoon vanilla
1½ cups chopped nuts
    (optional)

Butter baking pan, 8x8x2 inches. Heat milk, chocolate chips and unsweetened chocolate in 2-quart saucepan over low heat, stirring constantly, until chocolate is melted and mixture is smooth. Remove from heat; stir in vanilla and nuts. Spread mixture evenly in pan. Refrigerate until firm. Cut into 1-inch squares. 2 POUNDS CANDY (64 SQUARES).

Candy lovers everywhere savor the special attractions of holiday candies. This is the window of a Boston sweet shop at Eastertime.

PENUCHE

1 cup granulated sugar
1 cup packed brown sugar
⅔ cup milk
2 tablespoons corn syrup
¼ teaspoon salt

2 tablespoons butter or
    margarine
1 teaspoon vanilla
½ cup coarsely chopped
    nuts (optional)

Butter loaf pan, 9x5x3 inches. Heat granulated sugar, brown sugar, milk, corn syrup and salt to boiling in 2-quart saucepan over medium heat, stirring constantly, until sugars are dissolved. Boil, stirring occasionally, until candy thermometer registers 234° (or until small amount of mixture dropped into very cold water forms a soft ball that flattens when removed from water). Remove from heat; stir in butter. Cool, without stirring, to 120° or until bottom of saucepan is lukewarm.

Add vanilla. Beat with wooden spoon until mixture is thick and no longer glossy, 5 to 10 minutes. (Mixture will hold its shape when dropped from spoon.) Stir in nuts quickly. Spread mixture evenly in pan. Cool until firm. Cut into 1-inch squares. 1 POUND CANDY (32 SQUARES).

Sweets **155**

SUGARPLUMS

1 package (15 ounces) raisins
8 ounces dried apricots (about
   1½ cups)
8 ounces dried figs (about 1⅓
   cups)

8 ounces pitted prunes (about
   1⅓ cups)
1 cup pecans or walnuts
   (optional)
Sugar (optional)

Chop all ingredients except sugar in food grinder, using coarse blade; mix thoroughly. Shape mixture by rounded teaspoonfuls into balls. Roll in sugar. Let stand uncovered until dry, about 4 hours. Refrigerate in tightly covered container.   ABOUT 7 DOZEN CANDIES.

Fruit Bars: Press mixture evenly in buttered baking pan, 13x9x2 inches. Cut into bars, about 3x1 inch. Wrap in plastic wrap or waxed paper.   32 CANDIES.

CANDIED GRAPEFRUIT PEEL

2 large grapefruit
Water

About 2½ cups sugar

Score grapefruit peel into sixths with sharp knife. Remove peel carefully with fingers. Scrape white membrane from peel with spoon (back of peel will appear porous when membrane is removed). Cut peel into strips ¼ inch wide. Heat peel and 8 cups water to boiling in 3-quart saucepan; reduce heat. Simmer uncovered 30 minutes; drain. Repeat process 3 times.

Heat 2 cups of the sugar and 1 cup water to boiling in 2-quart saucepan, stirring until sugar is dissolved. Add peel. Simmer uncovered, stirring occasionally, 45 minutes. Drain thoroughly in strainer. Roll peel in remaining sugar; spread on waxed paper to dry.   ABOUT ⅓ POUND CANDY.

Candied Orange Peel: Substitute 3 large oranges for the grapefruit. Simmer in water twice.

Food photography director: George Ancona

Other photographs: Title page — Len Weiss (left), Subli/Photo Trends (center), R. T. Cook/Contemporary Color (right); page 8 — Grant Heilman; page 16 — Brian Seed/Black Star; page 37 — Bob McNerling/Taurus Photos; page 54 — Grant Heilman; page 64 — Harry Gruyaert/Woodfin Camp Assoc.; page 70 — Brian Seed/Black Star; page 75 — Todd Tarbox/EPA; page 82 — George Ancona; page 92 — Brian Seed/Black Star; page 97 — Ted Spiegel/Black Star; page 102 — John Running/Stock Boston; page 108 — George Ancona; page 114 — Michael Philip Manheim; page 129 — Grant Heilman; page 134 — Grant Heilman; page 145 — Gordon Baer/Black Star; page 149 — Dunn/DPI; page 155 — George Ancona.